Tantric Sex

Ancient Hindu Practice to Expand Your Sexual Energy, Experience Mind-Blowing Sex and Overcome Taboo of Kama Sutra. Level up Your Sex Life and Learn Tantric Massage.

© **Copyright 2019 by Eva Harmon - All rights reserved.**

The content contained within this book may not be reproduced, duplicated or transmitted without direct written permission from the author or the publisher.

Under no circumstances will any blame or legal responsibility be held against the publisher, or author, for any damages, reparation, or monetary loss due to the information contained within this book. Either directly or indirectly.

Legal Notice:

This book is copyright protected. This book is only for personal use. You cannot amend, distribute, sell, use, quote or paraphrase any part, or the content within this book, without the consent of the author or publisher.

Disclaimer Notice:

Please note the information contained within this document is for educational and entertainment purposes only. All effort has been executed to present accurate, up to date, and reliable, complete information. No warranties of any kind are declared or implied. Readers acknowledge that the author is not engaging in the rendering of legal, financial, medical or professional advice. The content within this book has been derived from various sources. Please consult a licensed professional before attempting any techniques outlined in this book.

By reading this document, the reader agrees that under no circumstances is the author responsible for any losses, direct or indirect, which are incurred as a result of the use of information contained within this document, including, but not limited to, — errors, omissions, or inaccuracies.

Table of Contents

Introduction..5
Chapter 1: The Philosophy of Tantric Sex..7
Chapter 2: The Difference Between Sex and Tantric Sex..16
Chapter 3: The Need for Tantric Sex..............25
Chapter 4: Setting the Scene..........................34
Chapter 5: Fostering Intimacy and Touching...43
Chapter 6: Breathing and Relaxation.............52
Chapter 7: Using Toys.....................................60
Chapter 8: Exercises During Tantric Sex...69
Chapter 9: Positions During Tantric Sex........78
Chapter 10: Massages During Tantric Sex...86
Chapter 11: What is Tantric Pleasure?...........94
Chapter 12: The Male Orgasm.......................103
Chapter 13: The Female Orgasm...................112
Chapter 14: Individual Ecstasy......................120
Chapter 15: Couples Ecstasy..........................129
Conclusion..139

Introduction

Welcome to tantric sex. If this is your first time with tantra and the power it can bring to your sex life, then you don't know what you have been missing. You are in for a real treat. After reading this book, you will never go back to your old sex life ever again.

This book is about the art of tantric sex and how it can be used to increase your sexual energy to the limit of your capabilities. You will find that true, tantric experience is truly mind-blowing. When you reach the heights of sexual pleasure and ecstasy, you will become a completely different person. In fact, don't be surprised if you discover a whole new way of looking at life.

Now, this book is not a mere collection of sex positions and boring role plays. Those are just games. This book is meant to be your pathway to a life-altering experience that will leave you profoundly changed. It will make you and your partner achieve new levels of sexual connection, unlike you have ever felt.

Be prepared to challenge everything you have seen and heard about tantra. In these pages, you will find everything you need to know about making your sex life everything you have wanted it to be. So, if you thought you knew about tantra, prepared to be blown away... literally.

But don't worry if you haven't experienced tantra before. This book is meant to take you through a gradual process in which you will discover your own sexual energy and combine it with your partner. You'll find that the powerful connection that is created can lead to unbelievable heights of pleasure.

If you have experienced tantra in the past, then you have an idea of just how powerful it can be. However, this book will challenge your current perceptions and take you to the next level. As you go further in this book, you will uncover new levels that never knew were there.

So, the time has come to uncover the wonderful and magical side of tantric sex. The time has come to explore your sexuality and discover your partner's own desires and fantasies. Together, you can take things to the level which you have always wanted to.

However, there is one word of caution: the concepts, ideas, practices, and techniques in this book build on each other gradually. This means that if you, or your partner, are new to tantra, it's best to take it easy at first. It's important to take your time as tantra is not something that you can use right out of the box. It takes some time before you can truly master it. But when you do, you, there will be no turning back. Your partner, or partners, will look to you as "the one."

Let's get started on this journey to a world you have always wanted to explore, but perhaps didn't have the chance to. So, here it is. Here's your chance to make your sex life everything you have wanted it to be.

Chapter 1: The Philosophy of Tantric Sex

Sex is an important part of our lives. Regardless of your preferences and/or orientations, sex is a vital component to making our lives full and complete. Without it, it can be quite difficult to lead a healthy and productive life. In fact, the longer you go without it, the harder it can be to function properly in life.

Now, it should be noted that there is a difference between sex and tantric sex.

Regular, run of the mill sex (which we will be referring to as "traditional sex") is an act which virtually all humans go through at some point in their lives. Unfortunately for some, they go through traumatic experiences with sex. This is something that cannot be disregarded and has an important place in tantra.

How so?

Well, sex is about a physical, emotional, and psychological experience that is meant to take us to heights of pleasure, intimacy, and connection. Sex is about connecting with your partner (or partners, as the case may be) in such a way that you are able to mutually satisfy each other. This mutual satisfaction can lead to a connection that brings out the best in both of you.

Of course, there is a place for love and romance. But as far as this book is concerned, love and romance are a separate topic. The reason for this is that love and romance are not pre-requisites to having a magical experience with tantric sex. In fact, you can conjure up an amazing experience with someone you have barely met. This is possible if you know what you are doing.

Moreover, tantric sex differs from traditional sex in the sense that you are focusing on both yourself and your partner. This is the crux of the matter. If you are selfish and don't pay close attention to your partner's needs, then your sexual encounter won't result quite as good as you might have hoped for.

In fact, if you're plan is to get off and have a merry old time, then tantric sex may not be the most effective philosophy for you. If you're just looking for fun and creative ways to spice up your sex life, then you'll be quite surprised to find that tantric sex goes far beyond that.

When you are committed to making your own sexual experience the best it can be by making your partner's experience as good as it can be, then you know you're in the tantra ballpark. Please bear in mind that this isn't about looks, size, or stamina; this is about knowing what buttons to push and when to push them. Master that, and you will forever go down in history as one of the best.

If that seems like an outrageous claim, don't worry. Once you see what tantric sex can do, especially to someone who hasn't really experienced it before, you'll frame this page up on your wall.

Defining tantric sex

Sadly, most so-called gurus and sexperts pass off tantric sex for a collection of funky positions that don't really anywhere. Sure, it can be fun to try out some new positions, but at the end of the day, if you don't add all of the components that make up a tantric session, then you will be coming up short.

Tantric sex can be viewed as focusing on slow intercourse. This isn't about banging away until everyone comes. In fact, orgasm is not the main focus on tantra.

Does that seem surprising?

If you are unfamiliar with tantric sex, then it surely does seem surprising.

Tantric sex is about synchronizing movements, breathing, eye contact, touching, and even orgasms... it's all about taking your partner and leading the way. As your partner follows along, you can connect with them in such a way that everything moves in concert. Each movement, thrust, breath, touch, and so on, is done with a clear intention in mind.

Of course, there is always room for a quick romp.

But that's not what tantra is about. Tantra is about finding the right place and the right time to get it on. If you are in a hurry, then tantra's not for you. You need to focus and take your time. Otherwise, you won't be able to hit the heights you expect.

Tantric sex and love

If you are planning to engage in tantric sex with a loving and committed partner, you will find that your sexual encounters will become unforgettable. Tantra becomes easier when you have a history with your partner in such a way that you are both comfortable with each other and have a high degree of trust.

However, this doesn't mean that you have to be in love with them.

As a matter of fact, it is quite common to find tantra practitioners who hook up just because they know they are going to be in for a real treat. When two experienced practitioners get together, fireworks light up. As such, you don't need to be in love with your partner, though it certainly helps if you are.

It should also be said that tantric sex isn't really a one-night stand type of thing. If you believe that you can hook up with someone on a random night and have a mind-blowing tantra session, then you might be disappointed.

Ideally, tantra works with someone you know, someone you trust and with whom you can build a connection. That is something which you can't really do with someone you meet at a club or a bar. Often, it takes some time to get to know someone before you can really go through the roof in a tantra session.

Tantric sex is a mindset

When you really get into tantric sex, you'll find that it's mostly a question of mindset. When your head is not in the game, tantra doesn't work. You see, tantra is about making your energy flow. When this energy flows, it's like an electric charge that pulsates through your body. As this charge courses through your entire being, your partner will pick up on that. As your partner's energy flows as well, then a circuit is complete. This circuit enables the energy to flow through both of you.

That is why tantra isn't about orgasm; it's about prolonging the experience as much as possible. But that doesn't mean that you have to go for hours. In fact, those who master tantra are quite efficient at achieving orgasm (we'll be defining that in a bit).

That being said, tantric sex isn't about spending hours in bed. It can be something as short as 10 or 15 minutes. But even if it's just 15 minutes, if your mind is really into it, you can achieve pleasure that will literally blow you away.

Please keep in mind that focus is key. You can't expect to have a full tantric experience while you are concerned about this thing or that thing. Most experienced tantra practitioners find that disconnecting while in a tantra session is a means of release. So, turn off your phone and forget about emails. When you are ready for a tantric session, the world around you goes away. All you need to focus on is you and your partner.

In a manner of speaking, tantra is like mindfulness. Mindfulness is about focusing on the "here" and the "now." This is why you will hear tantra experts say that tantra is like meditating. And when you truly think about, that's what it is. Tantric sex is like meditating on your sexual energy.

The slower, the better

One of the worst things modern culture has taught people is that fast and hard are the "hottest" ways to have sex. You often see that in movies, TV shows, and books. Perhaps the worst of all is pornography. Most porn films feature fast and aggressive movements that don't really foster any kind of connection. After all, porn is just acting.

This is the main reason why porn is so damaging to those who believe that real sex is like porn films. When you break it down, going as hard as you can, while exciting to a certain degree, does not foster the connection and intimacy that is needed to achieve real tantric ecstasy.

Consequently, the phrase, "the slower, the better" ought to become your new mantra. If you get it in your head that taking your time is the way to go, then you will find that opening the door to tantra is quite easy.

Of course, going slow can be hard for some, especially men. For guys, it can be hard to go slow, and controlling arousal and orgasm can be a real challenge. This is why tantra is not something you can just read through and put it to use. Tantra is the type of practice that needs time and dedication.

But there is some good news. The practices we will outline throughout this book will help those who have trouble controlling their arousal find the means of settling down and allowing their energies to really flow. This is why the mantra, "the slower, the better" will make all the difference in the world.

Taking the leap

Now that we have defined what tantric sex is all about, you are ready to take the leap into the world of pleasure. So, to kick things off, make a concerted effort to put your current way of looking at sex behind you. Now, make a conscious decision to embrace a new way of looking at sex. This new way is based on being open-minded. When you are truly open-minded, you are open to the new experiences you are about to encounter.

Please don't think we're talking about bondage or that sort of thing (well, if you're into it...) We're talking about being open-minded in such a way that you are focused on experiencing everything that sex has to offer you, everything from a wonderful physical experience to a deep, emotional connection. With that mindset, you can't go wrong.

If you are in a committed relationship, then please take the time to talk about this with your partner. Talk about what you expect from your sex life. By talking about it, you can both be on the same page. This will allow your tantric sessions to be focused on what fulfills you.

For instance, some couples value touching and kissing a lot more than penetration. Other couples place a higher emphasis on rhythmic movements as if they were dancing. Other couples value the sensory perception of their encounters above everything else. A good example of sensory perception can be scents or sounds that are arousing or soothing.

As you can see, there really is no "standard" way of enjoying tantra. There isn't some formula that you need to follow. Sure, there is a path you must go down, but at the end of the day, this path leads to different outcomes. In fact, don't be surprised to find that practicing tantra with different partners leads to completely different results. Naturally, everyone is different, so it's logical to assume experiences will be different, too.

So, here is your first exercise: the next time you have intercourse with your partner, try to set the stage so that you have no interruptions or distractions. This means no phones, no gadgets, no nothing. If you must get away somewhere, then do it. It could even be just booking a hotel room in your city. The point is to devote your entire time and attention to your partner, even if it's just a couple of hours. The secret here is to give your undivided attention to what you want and what you want to give your partner. That alone is enough to make your next sexual encounter a great one. So, please get into the habit of blocking out the world around you and focusing your energies and

One of the most interesting dynamics of traditional sex is the need for domination and/or control. Sure, most couples have one partner who leads, and the other tends to follow along. But in the world of tantra, this isn't about having one partner dominate the other such as in the world of BDSM. The fact of the matter is that tantra practitioners don't seek power, domination, or control. What they seek is to please their partner, and as a result, themselves.

Now, that happens if you are naturally dominant? Does that mean that there is no place for you in the world of tantra?

That's hardly the case!

In fact, dominant individuals take great pleasure in guiding their partner through the road that leads to pleasure and ecstasy. This is the ultimate rush that a dominant individual can derive from tantra.

Think about that...

What could be better than blowing your partner's mind? Imagine how incredibly satisfying it can be to give your partner the best sex of their lives... this is a feeling you can't get from "dominating" your partner.

You see, in traditional dom-sub relationships, the dom derives pleasure from the power rush that comes from having their sub at their mercy. This is a one-way relationship in which the sub doesn't always derive pleasure from their position. In fact, there are many cases that subs go along with the game simply music or any other auditory stimulus, smell such as your favorite scents, touch such as massaging, and of course, taste (food and drink can also be part of the experience).

To put this into perspective, think of all the mating rituals that humans go through prior to hitting the sack. For example, dance is a powerful mating ritual. The most sensual dances mimic sexual movements in such a manner that they foster intimacy among the couple. When a couple is able to hit it off on the dance floor, they can be confident they can hit it off in bed. While this doesn't necessarily constitute a guarantee, it's a heck of a place to start.

Another powerful mating ritual is food. This is the reason why most dates (especially first dates) involve food in one way or another. Also, drink plays a vital role in mating rituals. Just look at films and TV shows. Most dates begin with dinner and drink, and then end up in the sack. The sensory perception that is built with food and drink carries over into coitus.

So, if you are keen on really getting a full, tantric experience, don't skimp on the entire event leading up to sex. While it is not necessary for you to put together an elaborate evening, it is certainly helpful if you set the stage in this manner. This can be especially helpful while you learn the ways of tantric sex. Eventually, you won't need such an elaborate setup.

Difference #3: There is no domination or control

even seems transactional to a certain degree. That is why sex is much more than just reaching orgasm. It's about the entire experience surrounding the encounter.

For a lot of women, reaching orgasm can be a challenging endeavor. Often, this is due to the lack of synchronicity with their partner. There are times when it seems that there is no communication whatsoever. When this happens, one partner gets off, and the other... may not.

That is why the entire scene that surrounds tantra begins well before actual coitus. It begins with both partners fostering intimacy. It begins with being in touch with each other's needs and desires. From there, the overall experience of the encounter makes sex much more enjoyable. At that point, orgasm is a natural consequence. For women, this can lead to multiple orgasms. And, believe it or not, it can also lead to multiple orgasms for men (yes, that's right!)

Difference #2: It's a sensory experience

Sex goes beyond the mere act of intercourse, be it through penetration, touching, or oral. It involves all of the senses in such a manner that everything works in sync. When all senses are involved in a single encounter, the sensory experience is much broader.

This is what leads to the mind-blowing experience.

When you are committed to a full sensory experience, you begin sex with visuals such as dressing up (whatever you fancy is perfectly fine), sounds such as

Even if you have intercourse ten times a day, the energy is stuck there within you. Your sexual energy is never released unless you give it the time it needs to fully unfold and envelope you. When you are open to such experiences, you allow your core to absorb every minute detail of intercourse.

In this chapter, we are going to explore five important differences between traditional sex and tantric sex. These differences will enable you to have a crystal-clear understanding of what tantric sex and what it can do to improve your sexual life exponentially.

So, let's get right into it.

Difference #1: It's not about orgasm

When most folks think about sex, they see orgasm as the ultimate goal. This is particularly true for most men. Most guys tend to believe sex begins with arousal and ends with orgasm. In between, there is intercourse. However, intercourse is just a means to an end, so to speak.

This mentality is detrimental to a healthy and fulfilling sex life as sex, itself, is much more than the mere act of intercourse. In a manner of speaking, it's like reducing a meal to just dessert. So, instead of enjoying every bit of food in your meal, you simply rush through the first course just to get to dessert. Once dessert is served, you wolf it down and be done with it.

When you look at sex in this manner, you won't ever truly enjoy everything it has to offer you. In fact, it

Chapter 2: The Difference Between Sex and Tantric Sex

At the beginning of our sex lives, we don't really know what to do or what to expect. Even when your parents give you "the talk," you really don't know what's happening until you actually do it. Then, depending on the amount of sex education you get, you learn more and more about sexuality and how it actually works.

However, most people don't really take the time to learn as much as they can about sex. It's funny that we should act in this manner, especially since sex is such a significant part of human life. In fact, most of what we learn is generally on the fly. For example, you hook up with someone who's older and more experienced, they show you what to do, and that's that.

For some guys and gals, teaching a virgin about sex is a thrill they relish. Then, there are some who are caring and strive the show a younger partner how to really enjoy. Sadly, these people and experiences are hard to come by.

That is why your interest in this book is a testament to your desire to learn about the best ways in which you can unleash your sexual potential. Through the art of tantric sex, you can unlock all of the repressed energy within you.

Yes, that's right, repressed energy.

attention on your partner and nothing else. It's totally worth it!

because they want to feel "loved" in some way. As such, subs comply with their dom's bidding with the hope of gaining the dom's favor.

While this type of dynamic works perfectly well for some couples, it's not the type of relationship that is built for mutual pleasure and fulfillment. This is one of the reasons why dom-sub relationships tend to run their course; that is, they aren't meant to be long-term relationships.

With tantric sex, the focus is on mutual satisfaction and fulfillment. This implies that all parties have the chance to get what they want out of the relationship. Now, it should be noted that "relationship" doesn't mean a romantic partnership. If anything, a tantric relationship can be strictly sex with no strings attached. But the relationship and the dynamic that evolves from the practice of tantra can lead to a relationship that is far more fulfilling than your run-of-the-mill romantic partnership.

Difference #4: Nothing else matters

This is one of the biggest mistakes that couples make: they let other things get in the way during their encounters. Please bear in mind that tantric sex is about the here and the now. So, when you are getting it on, nothing else matters.

This concept doesn't apply just to phones and email. It also applies to anything else that might be creeping up in your mind.

For example, if you are concerned about your physical appearance, say, you're concerned about being overweight, then you will find that you won't be able to get as much out of your encounters as you'd like. Based on this concept, you really, truly, need to let go.

So what if you're not physically perfect?

So what if you're not the biggest?

So what if you're not the most attractive?

If you are attractive and desirable to someone who is willing to engage in tantric sex with you, then it's just a matter of going with it. In the end, you'll enjoy the relationship far more simply because you are able to let go of your hang-ups.

The fact of the matter is that we get in our own way. Most of the time, there is genuine attraction and chemistry. But when you don't give yourself a chance to really enjoy intercourse, then you find your mind more concerned about a million other things. Needless to say, this isn't the most exciting mindset.

The overwhelming majority of tantra practitioners would much rather get with someone who shares their same mindset rather than someone who's merely good-looking. This means that tantric sex is much more than just looking good; it's about being able to translate your passion and desire into a tangible force that can open up the floodgates to amazing experiences of pleasure and ecstasy.

Difference #5: Surrender at all times

By "surrender," we're not talking about some kind of domination thing. We're talking about letting yourself go and giving yourself to your partner. This is the core tenet of tantric sex. You must be willing to give all of yourself, even for a brief moment, before you are truly able to channel your energy into the powerful force that tantric sex can unleash. If you are holding back, then you won't be able to fully harness your sexual energy.

If you are a more submissive person by nature, this might be easier to achieve. By nature, you don't need to be in control. So, it's far easier to simply go with it. But for naturally dominant individuals, surrendering may represent a monumental challenge.

Surrender happens at various levels. Firstly, anyone who engages in sexual intercourse (unless it is against their will) surrenders physically. Often, folks think this is the last thing you surrender.

That could not be farther from the truth!

Surrendering your body in the act of passion is one of the easiest things you can do. It's surrendering everything else that becomes the hardest part.

As such, the next level, the emotional level, is paramount to tantric sex. Again, we are not talking about "love" here. Love has nothing to do with tantric sex. While it certainly helps to love your partner (it certainly facilitates the process), what you really need is to be emotionally invested in what you are doing. This implies that you need to be ready to give this person all of the care and attention they need during your encounter.

This is what fosters intimacy.

Then, the third level becomes a deep, spiritual level. When you are able to achieve this level, you are able to really hit it out of the park. Your connection is so profound that mind-blowing sex becomes a regular occurrence. Again, love is not a pre-requisite. But a deep understanding of each other's wants and needs is.

So, take it upon yourself to be ready to give all of yourself to your partner, even if it is for the brief moment you are together.

Chapter 3: The Need for Tantric Sex

Throughout this book, we have talked about how important sex is in the life of humans. After all, if sex wasn't important, then there wouldn't be so much attention paid to it. It would go practically unnoticed. If anything, it would serve for reproductive purposes, and that would be the end of it.

The fact that sex is so important in our lives forces us to make sex as enjoyable as possible. That's where tantra really shines. Tantra is all about situating sex in its rightful place. By giving sex the importance it deserves, you can lead a much more satisfying and fulfilling life.

In this chapter, we are going to be taking a closer look at the need for tantric sex. Now, we're not just talking about sex in general; we're talking about tantric sex. And yes, there is a clear need for it. There is a clear need for having the best possible sexual experience of your life. If you believe that tantric sex is just about massages and playing soft music, then do read on.

Sex is meant to be enjoyable

In popular culture, sex is objectified to a degree in which it is seen as a transactional occurrence. For instance, sex is used as a currency in order to obtain benefits from people. In addition, sex is reduced to a mere physical act in which one, or hopefully both, of the parties involved, get a physical rush out of it. If you are more adventurous, group sessions (or sex with multiple partners) is seen as some type of thrill that doesn't really lead anywhere.

This is where people end up feeling shallow and empty. Sure, they may be sleeping with very attractive people, but at the end of the day, they don't get as much fulfillment out of it as they would expect. In fact, this is where you see extremely attractive people debase themselves simply because they don't enjoy intercourse.

Then, you have committed and/or monogamous relationships. There are folks who view sex as a chore in such relationships. So, sex isn't about having a great time with their partner. Rather, sex is viewed as a necessary evil in the relationship. Under these circumstances, you can't expect sex to be fulfilling. At best, it would be able to provide physical release. But the reality is that sex under those terms would only prove to be a monotonous event.

So, what can be done about it?

If you find yourself not enjoying your current sex life, then you really need to ask yourself: what do I want to get out of my sex life?

This question will lead you down a path in which you must explore what you really want to get out it. If you view sex as a currency that will get you everything you want, then tantric sex might not be right for you. However, if you view sex as something pleasurable that you would love to share with your partner (whoever that might be), then tantric sex is a must in your life.

Additionally, a healthy sex life is part of a well-rounded lifestyle. When you have a satisfying sex life, you can be sure that this will rub off on other areas of your life as well. So, there is no reason why you shouldn't strive to incorporate tantric sex into your life right away.

Traditional sex gets old... fast

Traditional sex is fun and exciting whenever you have a new partner in your life. Even the same old positions and routines become hot and steamy when you are in lust for someone. During this phase, a quick romp is enough to get your blood boiling. However, if there is no substance to your encounters, that passion can quickly fizzle out, leaving you with mundane encounters. This is why many relationships don't survive for too long.

Of course, it's true that relationships aren't solely about sex. There are other components surrounding sex which make relationships more or less enjoyable. For instance, if you and your partner share the same pursuits, then you can be sure that your relationship outside the bedroom will be fun, too. But if things aren't working as well as they could in the bedroom, then there will always be something missing.

When you look at traditional sex for what it is, physical enjoyment and attraction are the only things that can keep you coming back for more. When attraction wears off, then there had better be something else to your relationship.

This is where tantric sex makes all the difference.

When you engage in tantra, you are moving beyond physical attraction. You are moving into a realm of emotional and even spiritual enjoyment. While you could theoretically achieve this with anyone you meet, the truth is that it doesn't happen with just anyone. It takes two people (or perhaps more...) who are willing to surrender to each other during the time they are together.

Please keep this in mind at all times!

Surrendering yourself to your partner will allow you to open the floodgates of your sexual energy. Sure, there is heightened physical pleasure that comes from tantric encounters. But the fact is that the physical response is expanded by the non-physical components that are involved. In the end, the physical enjoyment you are able to get out of a tantric session will leave you feeling full. It's kind of like taking your time to savor your favorite food. In the end, you have not only enjoyed your meal but also satisfied your hunger. Ultimately, this leaves you with an amazing feeling.

Good sex is key to a healthy life

Multiple studies have shown the importance that sex has in our day to day lives. For example, sex can boost mood and improve cognitive performance. This is due to the release of chemicals by the brain after a satisfying sexual encounter.

Those studies are based on traditional sex, that is, people who engage in a "regular" sexual relationship. Now, if traditional sex can do that, imagine what tantric sex can do for you. In essence, what tantric sex does is help you circulate your sexual energy. When this occurs, it's like a wave of electricity that begins to power various aspects of your mind and body.

When you don't have sex, or you simply "get off," you don't allow your sexual energy to circulate through your body. This is why tantra calls for you to take your time. The more you rush a sexual encounter, the less chance you give your energy to flow.

According to ancient beliefs, sexual energy is located at the base of the spine. From there, it moves up your spine and circulates throughout your body. And while this is an automatic process, it doesn't happen automatically.

Wait a minute...

You see, when you don't take the time to release your energy, you exert physical energy through the mechanical act of coitus, but you don't give your sexual energy the chance to get moving and flow upward. As such, the mere act of reaching orgasm doesn't necessarily imply that your sexual energy is flowing to the maximum of its capabilities.

Here's how this works:

For men, sexual pleasure is equated with ejaculation. If a man ejaculates, this implies orgasm, and all is good. However, this belief is hardly ironclad. Any guy will tell you that ejaculation does not necessarily mean orgasm. While it may feel good, it doesn't necessarily mean that a man has reached the climax of sexual pleasure.

The reason for this is that an orgasm is a chemical process that goes on in the brain. When a person reaches sexual climax, the brain floods the body with pleasure-causing chemicals. When these chemicals are released, they flow through the bloodstream and feed all of the organs and body systems. In fact, orgasm causes the penis to get harder and not softer.

Think about that for a moment…

For a man to reach orgasm, he needs to focus more on the action that is happening, on his partner's pleasure and, of course, his own. This means that he cannot be focused on how good it feels and that he can't finish too soon.

This is where he needs to let go!

He needs to forget that he is feeling pleasure and focus on the here and now. That can open the door to the chemical reactions that are produced as a result of pure sexual pleasure. In the end, a man who can master this mindset may find himself having multiple orgasms well before ejaculating once.

As for women, orgasm is a mix of emotions, physical sensations, and a sense of security. When you combine all of these elements, it's possible to reach unbelievable heights of sexual pleasure. However, women can be betrayed by their emotions. For example, if a woman feels uncomfortable about anything surrounding the encounter (such as feeling guilty about it), reaching orgasm can be quite difficult. By the same token, if she feels insecure about her physical appearance, this can also lead her to have difficulty reaching orgasm.

Again, this is why tantra is about the here and the now. When a woman is able to focus on the "task at hand," so to speak, she can let herself go. This is an emotional response in which she isn't focused on what is happening in the world around her; she is only focused on what's happening between her and her partner. That's all that matters.

Making orgasms count

One of the most common misconceptions about tantric sex is that orgasms keep coming and coming. While that may be true for some people, the fact is that it doesn't quite work that way. For many couples, having one orgasm is more than enough to make the session memorable. This is why we say you should "make orgasms count." When you really make orgasms count, the overall sensation that comes with them is incredible.

Now, it may seem paradoxical, but if you aim to reach orgasm, then it will be harder for you to get there. So, your aim in a tantric session is not to reach orgasm. Your aim should be to just enjoy it. The orgasm will come when it comes.

Do you see the difference?

When your pursuit of a sexual encounter is orgasm, you will find that it's nearly impossible to get it. It's like when you're unemployed and in need of a job. If you get desperate, you will project that in job interviews. Plus, each day that passes without a job seems like an eternity. After just a few days of job hunting, you are so stressed out and anxious that you might even get sick.

The same goes for orgasms.

If you are fixated on reaching orgasm, you'll find it nearly impossible to focus on what you are actually doing. You won't be able to focus on enjoying your partner. If anything, it'll feel good up to a certain point, but nothing else.

On the flip side, if you choose to enjoy coitus for what it is, you'll find it's a lot easier to relax and let your energy flow. When you are able to do this, reaching orgasm comes naturally. As a man, you're not worried about finished too fast. That's why you're going slow. In the case of a woman, you're not concerned that it takes you forever to reach orgasm. All you're concerned about is enjoy each passing moment with your partner.

This is the core essence of tantric sex. All of the components that make up tantric sessions are building blocks to a wonderful experience. Consequently, everything you do, from dancing to massages, is a precursor to the big "O." That way, when the big "O" does arrive, you'll be ready to literally burst at the seams.

So, make every orgasm count by letting yourself go and surrendering to your partner.

Chapter 4: Setting the Scene

In tantric sex, setting the scene just right is as important as anything you do with your partner. Often, setting the scene is about setting up a comfortable atmosphere in which both of you can just be yourselves.

This is the main point here.

The right stage can make your tantric sessions that much more enjoyable. The proper atmosphere can turbocharge your senses, thereby making the overall experience memorable. In fact, having the right atmosphere alone is enough to take traditional sex into tantric territory.

But first, let's talk about what we don't mean by "setting the scene."

If you are picturing an elaborate situation in which your bedroom is flooded by candles and rose petals, then you might be taking things a bit too far. Sure, if that's the type of thing you are into, then so be it. However, you don't have to remodel your bedroom to set the right scene. If anything, you'll find that trying to hard to set the right stage will end up killing the mood altogether.

Here is a quick example:

Let's say that you want to surprise your partner with a truly special evening. So, you go pull all the stops to make your bedroom look like a scene out of a movie.

You have soft music playing in the background, champagne on ice, and even some visual stimulus on the television. While this scene may seem perfect, it could backfire as it creates pressure on your partner to deliver. After all, how would you feel if your partner surprised you in this way? You'd feel pressured to make it worth their while. Of course, we're not talking about a transactional relationship, here. But, you would still feel pressured not to disappoint your partner.

Based on this example, it's plain to see that taking things too far can create unnecessary pressure on your partner. The higher you set your expectations, the harder it will be for you to enjoy yourselves.

So, let's take a look at what you can do to set the scene just right.

Talk with your partner about what they want

First and foremost, talk with your partner about what you both want in the perfect setting. It could be that you both have very simple tastes. Perhaps the décor isn't as important as privacy. Moreover, you and your partner may value quiet and darkness more than a fancy setup.

Most couples who engage in tantric sex often set their ambiance to that of peace, quiet, and privacy. The main idea here is that whatever happens in the bedroom stays in the bedroom. The last thing tantra practitioners want to worry about is the neighbors overhearing them. If they have kids, they don't want to worry about what their kids are doing while they are getting it on.

As you can see, for most folks, setting the right scene isn't so much about the visuals of a room that looks right out of a magazine. For them, it's the peace and quiet that makes all the difference. This is why it is vital that you and your partner communicate your preferences to one another.

Setting up the right visuals

Visual stimulation is essential to fulfilling tantric sex. By "visuals," we mean everything that your eyes can possibly take in. This can range from the décor and ambiance to the actual physical appearance of you and your partner.

Regarding physical appearance, anything goes!

For instance, wearing sexy lingerie, costumes, or just wearing a birthday suit can provide you with the visual stimulation you seek. Some couples enjoy dressing up with a theme in mind. Others enjoy role plays. Some prefer watching racy films to set the mood. The fact of the matter is that anything goes so long as you are both on board.

This is important to keep in mind, especially because anything that makes you or your partner uncomfortable can become a mood killer. This is the last thing you want to see happen. As such, setting any and all visuals, as long as you are both comfortable, will go a long way toward making your tantric session memorable and enjoyable.

Taking in the sounds

This is a tricky one. The traditional playbook (such as what you generally see in films) calls for soft music or smooth jazz playing in the background. However, some folks find music, or any other sound, for that matter, to be distracting. So, this doesn't mean that they don't enjoy it; it's just that background sounds may lead them to become distracted from the actual encounter itself.

To put this into perspective, imagine this situation:

Suppose you are studying for a big exam. This is an important mid-term that you need to focus all of your mental energies on. So, do you study in silence or have music blasting in the background?

Your answer to this question should give you a clear indication of how you would react to music (or any other sound) during our tantric session. In fact, it could be that you enjoy having smooth jazz playing in the background. But your partner may not. So, this is where you need to strike a balance.

One common practice is to play music while things are heating up. This could be during a massage, kissing, touching, or just cuddling. But when it comes down to intercourse, the music is off. While this doesn't mean that you are going to be in absolute silence, it does mean that there aren't any other sounds that could potentially distract you from what's going on at the moment.

In fact, turning the music off is quite useful when you are syncing your breathing. You see, when there are other noises around, it can be hard to hear your breathing. As such, you might have a hard time syncing up. But when you don't have any distracting sounds around you, it's far easier to sync your breathing. This is especially true if you close your eyes and let your other senses take over.

One other thing about sounds: don't feel compelled to make a huge ruckus during sex. One very persistent misconception is that yelling your head off is a sign of enjoyment. While that might be true for some, there are plenty of folks (women, especially) who have a mind-blowing orgasm without feeling the need to scream their head off. So, if you, or your partner, aren't the screaming type, then that's perfectly fine. Everyone is different, and it's something we need to embrace.

Lighting to set the mood

This is another one of those tricky areas. Lighting can really set the mood for you and your partner, or it can throw a monkey wrench into your session.

The rule of thumb here is that there is no rule of thumb.

Some couples feel perfectly comfortable in a well-lit area, while others prefer darkness. Again, this is all about what makes you feel comfortable. As such, it's a question of being on the same page.

In this regard, some folks like to "see what they are doing." So, a well-lit area for them works perfectly fine. They don't mind having the lights or getting it on during the daytime. For other couples, they prefer the anonymity of darkness. Thus, you'll see them drawing blackout curtains during the daytime while perhaps leaving their environment pitch black at night.

As a matter of fact, you'll find that experience tantra practitioners prefer the dark as it cancels the visuals out and forces them to feel and hear everything they are doing. For some, it's hard to concentrate when there is a large amount of visual stimulation around them. For others who are a bit more self-conscious about their physical appearance, darkness gives them the opportunity to forget about the imperfections they perceive in their body.

Once again, this is a call that you ought to make as a couple. That way, you can both feel comfortable. In the end, it's one less thing to worry about.

Using scents to your advantage

Scents are paramount in tantra. The right scents can give you the chance to focus on a different kind of sensory perception. Scents are very useful when it comes to triggering positive emotions. This is why scents are practically a cliché during massages. Everything from scented candles to essential oils is highly recommended.

When selecting scents, it's important to choose ones that trigger positive emotions. For instance, your partner is nuts for chocolate ice cream. So, using chocolate-scented oils can work wonders during a massage. In other cases, essential oils such as lavender can provide you with the olfactory stimulation you seek, that is, entering a state of relaxation.

Now, here's one naughty trick you can use to get things started in a very discreet way. Pick a scent that you both find pleasing. It could be a perfume, cologne, essential oil, scented candle, even some kind of food. Then, set a rule that this scent is only used during sexual encounters. This is a type of code that indicates that you are ready to go over the moon.

Here's the trick: use the scent well before you actually get it on. This will signal your partner what you intend to do. Even if you are nowhere near the bedroom (or your chosen place), the scent is enough to begin triggering the emotions that you associate with intercourse. By the time you actually get "down to business," your mind and body will already be in a state of readiness. In a manner of speaking, you have gotten a head start on your pleasure.

Things don't always happen in the bedroom

If you believe that an amazing tantric session only takes place in your bedroom, then you might be surprised to find that tantric sex can happen anywhere! Yes, practically any place is good for a tantric session.

To choose a place for your sessions, it must meet your criteria. Otherwise, it wouldn't work at all. Now, when we say "criteria," it's a question of meeting your requirements in terms of lighting, mood, privacy, and so on.

This means that if your garage fits the bill, then your garage would be the place to be.

It's also important to keep in mind that lifestyles are quite varied. Some couples have very busy lifestyles and so on. That's why they seek to get away from it all to be together. So, some couples find hotel rooms or go on a trip somewhere to really get it on.

Ultimately, the actual location of where you do it doesn't really matter so long as it's a place that works for you. When you find this place, then you have a huge head start. Having the right place and the right atmosphere is just as important as any of the practices you can do. In fact, you could be a master practitioner of tantra, but if the mood and ambiance aren't right, you'll find that your experience just won't be the same.

At the end of the day, tantra is a combination of factors. If any factor is off, for any reason, then you might find it hard to make the most of your sessions. That's why communication is key. If you and your partner are on the same page, you will find it much easier to make the most of your time together. Even if you are naturally dominant and your partner is naturally submissive, being able to communicate what you both want is an essential part of tantra.

A healthy and rewarding sex life is all about being able to connect with your partner at a profound level. This is where tantra can lead both of you to levels you may have only dreamed about. Perhaps it might seem far away at this point. But with some careful planning and an open mind, you'll find that anything is possible in the world of tantra!

Chapter 5: Fostering Intimacy and Touching

Not everything in sex is about intercourse. Sadly, in our culture, sex is reduced to some kind of penetration, that's all there is to it. As a matter of fact, a harmful myth that persists is the belief that sex isn't really "sex" unless there is some kind of penetration.

While this is certainly an important part of sex, it isn't the only part. There are so many things that can happen during an encounter. This is why you need to be aware of the various options at your disposal. Truth be told, some of the most exciting and steamy parts happen outside of traditional penetrative sex.

That's why this chapter is centered on intimacy and touching. The main point is to focus on foreplay, or perhaps post-coitus activity. This is very important to keep in mind as there are so many things that can happen before and after intercourse.

Fostering intimacy

Intimacy isn't just the act of sex itself. Intimacy is an emotional connection that is felt between two individuals (or more as the case may be). You can potentially develop an intimate emotional connection with anyone without being in a committed relationship or being "in love." In fact, our lives are filled with intimate connections, such as those we cherish with family and friends. These types of intimate relationships have nothing to do with sex. It's the emotional connection that counts.

As such, it should be noted that the cornerstone of tantric sex is intimacy. Without it, achieving the truly uplifting heights of ecstasy can be hard to come by. While it is not impossible, it will take some additional effort to get there.

Fostering intimacy is not nearly as hard as you might think. The biggest step you can take with your partner(s) is to be honest about what you want, your expectations, and what you bring to the table. By being transparent in your intentions, you will find an unmatchable sense of liberation. It is so much more fulfilling to have an intimate relationship with some who you really connect with as opposed to someone with whom you have a superficial interaction.

This is the reason why mind-blowing tantric sex with a stranger is not quite that easy. It is possible if both parties are experienced in the ways of tantra. In that case, it might be quite easy for both parties to let go and surrender to the moment they find themselves in.

If you are in a committed relationship, intimacy is something that you ought to work on all the time. There are a plethora of activities that you can do to foster intimacy without even coming close to intercourse. When you make a concerted effort to foster intimacy in your day to day interactions, you will find that sex is just an extension of this usual interaction.

Building intimacy every day

Intimacy can be built every day through a clear and concerted effort to do so. For example, hugging, kissing, and meaningful touching (in a non-sexual way), is a great means of fostering intimacy.

Think about it for a minute.

If you don't even touch each other during the day, then how can you suddenly turn it on in the bedroom?

When you take the time to foster these kinds of interactions with your partner, you will find that playful touching, constant touching and kissing can easily transition into the bedroom. What you will find is that this type of behavior simply translates into sex without much effort. In a manner of speaking, you are ready for sex all the time.

Now, what happens if you are in a long-distance relationship?

In such cases, it's hard to build intimacy since you aren't physically present. This is where you need to get a bit more creative.

But before we get into it, a word of caution: if you plan to use photos and videos, please make sure that you are both on the same page about it. Unfortunately, photos and videos can fall into the wrong hands or can be misused, particularly when a relationship ends. So, it's important that all parties involved be on the same page.

That being said, the use of photos, videos, racy messages, or sexy calls over a webcam can really foster intimacy when physically separated. Please bear in mind that intimacy is more of an emotional and psychological phenomenon rather than a physical one. If anything, these types of exchanges tend to build up so much pressure that, by the time you are physically together, the fireworks are truly memorable.

In addition, building intimacy doesn't always involve racy content. Something as simple as being aware of your partner's needs on a regular basis can be enough to light a fire… and keep it burning.

The role of trust in building intimacy

When building intimacy, trust plays a key role. You have to trust your partner to some degree in order for you to be able to truly surrender yourself. This is something which can be hard when you don't really know someone.

By the same token, if there is an issue getting in between you and your partner, building trust can be quite complex. Without trust, achieving true tantric form can be more challenging. Given the fact that tantra is built on emotion and even spiritual connection, trust needs to be present at all times.

Now, it's important to note that we're not talking about trusting your partner with life and death decisions. This isn't about given them power of attorney. This is about trusting them enough to know that no harm will come to you while you are with them. This type of trust is so powerful that you know you won't have to worry about being hurt in any way. So, that leaves the door entirely open for you to relax and enjoy your encounter.

One of the biggest issues that pops up in committed relationships is infidelity. When one partner, or even both partners, are unfaithful, trust can be shot down. This drives a wedge between both partners in such a way that it may be nearly impossible to truly trust one another. As a result, this could make building your tantric experience somewhat more challenging.

If there is anything on your mind, it's best to talk about it with your partner. Get it out in the open. That way, you can clear the air and move on. That alone is enough to open the floodgates for most partners. It is incredible how unresolved issues can fester to the point where sex is no longer an enjoyable activity. In fact, sex may even become non-existent.

One other thing: it's important to discuss each other's limits. This is especially true if you are planning on engaging in some kind of BDSM activity. Trust needs to be put at the forefront of your mind. That way, you can be certain that your experience will be as pleasurable as you wish it to be. Please keep in mind that having sex with someone puts you in a vulnerable position regardless of whether you are a man or woman. So, the last thing that you want to have in mind is feeling insecure about anything that's going on during your encounter.

The power of touch

Touch is an incredibly powerful force. There is immaterial energy that is transmitted through touch. When you think about it, we can communicate so much more with a simply touching gesture than we could with words.

This is why handshakes are so important in business communication. When you go to business seminars, trainers often tell you that a handshake says much more about your character than your resume could ever say.

When it comes to sexual relationships, touch is a foundational element. You cannot expect to have the best sex of your life without incorporating touch in one way or another. However, not all touch is the same in the world of tantra.

Thus far, we have talked about the kind of touch you can do outside of the bedroom. This type of touch is great at fostering intimacy while keeping you "on your toes," so to speak. It's the type of silent communication between you and your partner that says you are always ready for action, even when you really aren't.

Now, most tantra books limit touching to sensual massages. And while we will be covering massages extensively, it's important to note that touch is so much more than that. Many times, light, sensual touching can produce unbelievable effects.

Using touch effectively

To heighten the sensation of touch, you really need to set the stage. This can be done through the atmosphere that we described earlier. In addition, hugging and cuddling can give you the opportunity to use touch effectively before you engage in actual intercourse.

Many couples enjoy genital touch, such as mutual masturbation, while cuddling and kissing. This is by no means meant to replace the entire act of coitus. However, it can be a power foreplay technique. All you need to do to make this technique effective is to relax and let go. In fact, many couples who have sex for the first time would rather spend a good deal of time touching well before engaging in intercourse.

Another important benefit of touching as part of foreplay is that it eases any anxiety prior to the main part of the show. This is important as genital stimulation allows you to become aroused at your own pace. Naturally, not everyone gets aroused in the same manner. For some, it takes longer than others. As such, touching can allow you to take all the time you need to get aroused at your own pace. That not only takes the pressure off, but it also allows you for variety.

Some tantra practitioners like to mix things up. For instance, they engage in intercourse and then separate in order to spend some time cuddling and kissing. This can be a good way of resting, particularly when you are planning to spend a good deal of time together.

Touching is incredibly useful, particularly for me. After ejaculation, there is a period in which the penis needs to recover before becoming erect again. This is a perfect time for touching. It's a way of keeping the party going without having to put additional pressure on having another erection right away. Furthermore, touching is incredibly powerful when one partner is essentially done while the other would like to keep going. As a matter of fact, some women report that they have more powerful orgasms following oral and manual genital stimulation (particularly stimulation of the clitoris) as compared to penetrative sex. While this may seem paradoxical, it actually makes sense. You see, when you are engaged in coitus with your partner, you are more focused on pleasing them rather than yourself. But when it's you that receives all the attention, it's far easier to just let go and enjoy the moment. This is when ecstasy can be taken to powerful heights.

As for post-coitus touching, please bear in mind that true tantric intercourse is a powerful event. This implies that simply shaking hands and being on your merry way doesn't really work. There needs to be some kind of touching, kissing, or just plain cuddling to bring your encounter to a natural conclusion. While cuddling after sex may not be your thing, at least acknowledging the fact that you had an amazing time is a great way of fostering intimacy. After all, you just had a great experience with some you enjoy being with.

So, do take the time to use touching as a cool down, so to speak. This will help you bring your encounter to a natural ending while leaving you connected with your partner even if you won't see them for a while. Please keep in mind that touch makes the experience all that more powerful while ensuring that you are building an intimate bond with this amazing person.

Chapter 6: Breathing and Relaxation

When it comes to tantric sex, being in sync is absolutely paramount to an effective session. When you and your partner move as one, each movement becomes that much more enjoyable. However, being in sync isn't something that happens automatically. It's something that takes some time and effort to develop.

In this regard, breathing is of vital importance. Breathing is not only useful when it comes to regulating physical exertion, but it's also the best tool that you can use to stay on the same track. You see, tantra looks for both partners to be going down the same path together. This implies that you are focused on where you and your partner are heading as opposed to focusing on your own path toward pleasure.

In this chapter, we are going to look at the role that relaxation plays in tantra and how you can achieve this through breathing. Plus, we're going to be focusing on how breathing is the ultimate road map which can lead you and your partner down the same path toward mutual pleasure and intimate connection.

The role of relaxation in tantra

There is no question that relaxation is essential in any good tantric session. Stress, anxiety, and distractions are the most common culprits of poor sex. These factors wreak havoc on libido and desire.

Just think about that for a moment.

You are trying to get your groove on, but you can't stop thinking about a problem you had at the office. Naturally, it's an important issue that's occupying your mind. And yes, you are eager to get with your partner and have a good time. However, your head is simply not in the game.

In the case of men, this leads to added pressure, which can result in trouble getting an erection. So, on top of the anxiety and stress at the start of the session, tension mounts, even more, when the pressure is on to perform. This can be a real mojo killer.

As for women, stress and overall anxiety can lead to trouble reaching orgasm. Sure, the session might be fun and enjoyable, but things just don't feel right. So, no matter how hard she tries, she just can't seem to get there.

If you have ever been in any of these situations, you can appreciate how tough it is to not only satisfy your partner but yourself. Needless to say, this does not make for an enjoyable romp in the bedroom.

So, what can you do about it?

The first thing to consider is being honest with your partner. If you let your partner know how you feel, they can help you settle down and relax. This is crucial as your partner is there to support you. They can help you calm down and enjoy your time together.

Nevertheless, that is easier said than done.

This is where breathing comes into play.

In addition to massaging, breathing is effective in relaxation. To use breathing as a relaxation technique, there isn't much that you need to do. One great exercise involves hugging and cuddling. You can sit on a sofa, lie in bed, or even stand. All you need to do is hold your partner (or be held) and simply breathe in unison. As you breathe, close your eyes and use your hands to "see" your partner's body. Don't be afraid to let your hands wander. If they should go to intimate places, then so be it! That's the whole point of the exercise.

One great way of incorporating structure into the exercise is to use rhythmic movements as if you were dancing. This could mean swaying from side to side or rubbing body parts such as the back, buttocks, genitals, breasts, or face. Each caress, each movement, each touch is intended to move in concert with each breath, that is, as you inhale and then exhale. Before you know it, you'll be moving in sync. This will eventually lead to arousal, which then leads to showtime.

Calming your mind

To say that your mind plays tricks on you is an understatement. When you are stressed out, anxious, or simply distracted, your mind gets the best of you.

Consequently, you don't have the freedom to enjoy sex as much as you would like.

In fact, it's quite easy to get caught up in any number of thoughts.

For instance, you can get caught up in your physical appearance. You might end up being too overly concerned about your body to the point where you can't really enjoy what you are doing. In fact, being insecure about your body (both and men and women) can lead you to feel bad, or even guilty, about sleeping with someone.

Your mind can also have a detrimental effect on your sex life when you let it run the show. This means that you can't let your mind get the best of you during sex. For example, you can't expect to have a mind-blowing session while you are analyzing what your partner is doing, what you should do next, or why things are happening the way they are.

Even though sex does call for careful thought and consideration, once you're in the bedroom, there is no need for sex to become a mathematical equation. Yes, you need to focus on what you are doing, but this doesn't mean you should be knit-picking everything that's happening.

As a matter of fact, if things aren't going right, you can always slow things down, spend some time touching, kissing, hugging or cuddling and regroup. If you can't trust your partner enough to take a time out and regroup, then perhaps you might be better off finding someone in whom you can confide.

So, here is a great exercise which you can do to calm your mind.

Now, whether you are actually having intercourse, or just getting warmed up, you can use your mind's eye to project what you want to happen. To do this, imagine that you're feeling a bright-colored light pulsating through your body. This light is coursing through every part of your being. It can start at the base of your spine and radiate onward. As you feel this energy flowing, imagine it is passing through to your partner at whatever point of contact you have. This could be through the hands, mouth, genitals, or any other point in which your bodies are in contact.

Next, imagine the light enveloping the both of you. Don't pay too much attention to the pleasure you are feeling. That will be there. It's something that you can't ignore. Just imagine the light connecting both of you. This light is the energy that you are sharing during your time together. Please keep in mind that there is no need for penetration to actually take place in order for this light to pass through the both of you. All energy needs is a channel which it can run through.

Now, here is the real kicker: as this energy, in the form of light, returns to you, what you are receiving is a recycled form of energy that isn't yours anymore. It belongs to the both of you. As this energy gets stronger and stronger, the pressure builds up in such a manner that when the big "O" comes, it's explosive. However, the big "O" does just end there. It's just a means of feeding the system in a closed-loop so that the pleasure keeps building and building, thereby leading to a stronger and stronger orgasm.

Syncing your breathing

In most tantra literature, you read about the importance of syncing your breathing. It should be noted that it isn't breathing per se that leads to connection. What leads to connecting with your partner is the fact that you are both moving in unison. The role breathing plays is to enable all parties involved to progress at the same rate or at the same pace.

To sync up your breathing, especially during intercourse, here is an effective exercise:

When you are in the midst of intercourse, you might find the action getting hot and heavy. As such, it's quite common for one partner to speed up while the other is moving along at a slower rate. It's important to remember that tantric sex is about taking things slow. This means that if your partner is racing along, you can slow the pace of the game down talking to them. Tell them to breathe in and breath out with you. You can help them by modeling the way they ought to be breathing. That way, you can slow things down and sync up your breathing.

As you get into the same rhythm, the actual speed of intercourse can move from a faster and more superficial tempo to a slower and deeper one. In fact, one highly effective practice is to mix things up. You see, when the rhythm of intercourse is fast and furious, it can't possibly last very long. It's just a matter of time before one, or both, simply explode and end up unable to recover. By the time they're ready again, the moment might have already passed.

So, when you mix things up, going fast and then slowing down, you will find that it gives you the chance to better manage your pleasure (and that of your partner's) while taking the time to savor the sights and feelings. If you are looking to take in the visuals, you will have enough time to feed your sight. If you are more inclined to the sensations of it all, you will have the time to savor the moment.

Now, if things appear to be getting out of control, don't be afraid to stop and regroup. Often, all it takes is a momentary pause to regain your breathing and then resume. Please keep in mind that experienced tantra practitioners are not afraid to take a breather even when the action is hot and heavy. In doing so, you can ensure that you are making the most of the time you are spending with your partner.

Don't forget to breathe!

For a lot of folks, breathing becomes an issue at the height of pleasure simply because they forget to breathe. Yes, as silly as that may sound, there are times when you might simply forget to breathe. This occurs because your entire nervous system is fixated on the pleasure you are feeling. However, when you stop breathing, you stop supplying oxygen to your body. Now, it's not like you are going to suffocate or anything. It's just that if you are looking to really enjoy your session, it's a good idea to be cognizant of your breathing.

Breathing is a great way to keep track of yourself. You see, when things are going really well, it's easy to get so caught up that you might end up losing yourself completely. While that is not a bad thing, it might cause you to neglect your partner. This is important, especially if you are very keen on pleasing your partner.

Consider this example:

As a man, it's easy to get caught up in the moment and lose control. When you lose control, you might feel compelled to finish. While this is not the issue, there might be an issue when your partner doesn't feel that they have gotten their fair share. For instance, the other partner hasn't reached their orgasm yet.

This situation exemplifies how breathing can help you stay in the moment. By focusing on breathing, both men and women can quell their mind, manage their emotions, and heighten their sensations. A simple way of using your breathing to your advantage is to simply focus on inhaling and exhaling. That's all. You don't need to count to ten, nor do you need to repeat some mantra in your mind. All you need to do is feel in the air entering your lungs and leaving your body. This alone is enough to get your body the oxygen it needs to perform up to the level you expect it to.

Chapter 7: Using Toys

One of the most common questions that surface with regard to tantric sex is the use of foreign objects, that is, "toys." Now, it should be noted that we're not talking about anything that could potentially cause harm such as artifacts used in BDSM. Also, we're not talking about any items that don't typically fall under the "sex toy" designation, such as sharp objects, machines, or even torture devices. In this discussion, we're talking about the types of things you would find in a regular sex shop such as dildos, vibrators, rings, plugs, beads, or even clamps.

Now, tantra purists will point out that textbook tantra doesn't call for the use of toys. If anything, toys can be considered as a distraction that can hinder reaching full tantric ecstasy. However, the use of toys can actually enhance pleasure particularly during a "warm-up," and especially during intercourse itself.

So, in this chapter, we are going to be discussing how you can incorporate the use of toys, should you choose to do so, under the scope of tantric sex. Moreover, we'll go over some recommended ways in which you can get the most out of the toys you bring into the bedroom.

Talking it over

Like anything in sex, the use of toys should be a mutual decision. These types of objects should not just be thrown into the mix. Sure, it might be a nice surprise, but if you haven't used toys before with a specific partner, it's always best to talk about it first.

For most women, the use of sex toys is not unheard of. In fact, you might be surprised to find most women are comfortable with the idea of using sex toys. After all, what's wrong with mixing things up a bit? The truth is that sex toys, like any other aspect of sex, are there to enhance enjoyment and pleasure.

For some men, the use of sex toys can actually be intimidating, especially if they have never used them before. This is due to the fact that the male ego may view the use of toys as a sign of dissatisfaction on the part of their partner.

This could not be farther from the truth.

A sex toy, no matter how good or pleasurable it may be, can never replace the type of interaction that comes with having sex with another person. As such, there is nothing to be worried about, or threatened by, when it comes to using sex toys.

That being said, it's important to discuss what types of toys you are both comfortable with. If you are new to the sex toy scene, perhaps you can start off with one and see how it goes. If you have had prior experience, you can talk about what you like and take it from there. By having an honest talk about what you like and what you would like to incorporate, you can ensure that your experience will be that much better.

Another important issue to talk about is boundaries. It is crucial to set your limits clearly. While you might be up for anything, there might be a certain thing you're not comfortable with, at least not yet. So, it's important to bring up these boundaries as this would avoid any potentially uncomfortable situations. The last thing you want to do is shut things down because you don't feel comfortable with anything. Please keep in mind that trust is an essential part of tantric sex.

Toys during warm-up

Prior to actual intercourse, you may choose to have a "warm-up" phase. This warmup portion of the program can be devoted to taking turns in giving and receiving pleasure.

This is where toys can really spice things up.

Consider this situation:

You are holding your partner while allowing your hands to touch all over your bodies. This touching is a great way of leading the way to arousal. Now, at this point, you might be inclined to focus on your partner's genital area. For the sake of this example, let's assume that it's a man who is stimulating a woman. The man's touch on his partner's genital area is soft and slow. The intent is to arouse his partner so that she can be receptive to intercourse.

At this point, rather than jumping straight into intercourse, why not try out a toy? For instance, a vibrator can be a perfect complement to the manual stimulation in the woman's genital area. This stimulation can go as far as you want it to go.

In fact, you can even try syncing your breathing while your partner is progressively becoming more and more aroused. While the man isn't necessarily receiving any direct stimulation, the emotional and psychological stimulation, that is, the sensory perception is a great way of boosting arousal. If you like, you can take your partner all the way to orgasm. In doing so, the woman can feel satisfied and fulfilled and... ready for more!

This example is a great way of aiding arousal. As such, toys can be used as precursors to the main event. Once in the main event, both partners can feel satisfied that they are thoroughly enjoying the situation.

Now, it should be noted that most sex toys are geared toward women. However, this doesn't mean that there aren't toys for men. It's worth taking the time to do research in order to find suitable toys based on a man's preferences. There are varying degrees of openness with regard to male sex toys, so if you're a man reading this, take some time to go through what toys are out there. If you're a woman reading this, you can peruse online catalogs with your man. That way, the experience of searching for sex toys can be a mutually bonding experience.

Toys during intercourse

The use of toys during intercourse is often debated. There are some who love the additional stimulation, while some dislike them completely. So, let's take a look at both sides of the argument.

For those who love toys during intercourse, these can provide additional stimulation. For instance, the use of clitoral vibrators during intercourse can provide another layer of arousal and stimulation. In fact, the combination of penetrative sex and clitoral stimulation can produce mind-bending orgasms. In a manner of speaking, it's like combining two foods that you love into one dish without them tasting weird.

Another facet of toys during intercourse is anal play. Some couples love using toys to stimulate the backside. This can also offer another layer of pleasure to the receiving partner. For women, anal stimulation during vaginal intercourse can produce an incredible sensation. And of course, there are men who also enjoy anal play during coitus even if they are heterosexual. Ultimately, the use of toys during intercourse is a question of finding the best way to get the most out of your experience.

On the flip side, there are those who dislike toys during intercourse altogether. The most common objection is that it becomes a distraction. For some, the use of toys during intercourse might mean fumbling in the dark for it. When looking at it from that perspective, it can certainly be seen as a distraction.

Additionally, some couples would rather not use toys during intercourse as they seek a unique experience in which it is them, and only them, who are involved in the action. While this is perfectly valid, it should also be noted that it ought to be a mutual decision. This implies that both parties should be on the same page. If one of the partners is reticent about using toys, they should at least give it a try. If they find that it's definitely not for them, then at least they gave it a try. However, it could be that once they try it, they can see just how good using toys can be.

How to determine if toys are right for you

There really is only one way to find out: try it!

If you don't try, at least once, to use toys during a tantric session, then you may never know if you are really missing out or not. It could be that you are missing out on a great experience without even knowing it. It might very well be that your hesitation about the use of toys is based on preconceptions that aren't really founded on anything.

Naturally, this argument is not intended to coerce you into trying out toys. Still, it's worth giving anything a shot at least once. In many cases, folks are reluctant to try toys out because they are afraid of being judged or seen negatively. The truth is that there is nothing wrong with the use of toys. It's just a natural part of human nature. If anything, denying yourself this opportunity can end up causing more harm than good.

Furthermore, if you commonly use toys during solo sessions (yes, both guys and gals use toys during solo sessions), then it only makes sense to carry that over into tantric sessions with your partner. As we have stated earlier, the use of toys is not about replacing your partner, or any other person for that matter, it's about enhancing the experience that you share with your partner.

Consequently, trying out toys is definitely worth a shot. If, after trying it, you feel it's not for you, then that's fair game. After all, tantric sex looks to push your boundaries. If you find yourself comfortably ensconced in your comfort zone, then you may be missing out on what could be one of the best experiences of your life.

Not all toys are created equal

It's also important to do your homework on the toys you plan to use. This is important as there is any number of toys out there. Some are rather straightforward, while others come in a variety of shapes, sizes, colors, textures, and functions. You can't really know what works for you until you try them out. So, it's always best to start off with the basics and move on from there. This is especially true when you haven't experimented with toys before.

When you go about purchasing your first sex toys, you might be tempted to make a big splash. However, you might not want to spend any big bucks until you are sure what's best for you. In fact, for most folks, simple works best. So, dishing out a pretty penny for the fanciest toys may not be the best choice, at least not at first.

Getting over the mental hang up

If you have no qualms about bringing toys into the bedroom, along with your partner, then make the most of your opportunity to enjoy a pleasurable experience with your partner... and some added stimulation.

However, if you are on the fence about bringing in toys, then it's worth going over the worst-case scenario. When you really think about it, what's the worst that can happen? If you really trust your partner, then there should be no reason why toys would get in the way. For instance, if you choose to try something out, but realize that it's not for you, or it didn't work the way you expected it to, then you can simply chalk it up to experience. If anything, it could be that you haven't chosen the right one.

Please keep in mind that this chapter isn't meant to convince you to use toys. It's meant to convince you to try new things. When you are truly committed to exploring the depths of tantra, you need to be prepared to open yourself up to new experiences. Otherwise, you will never get out of your comfort zone. As such, you may never be able to truly surrender yourself to your partner and the depths of pleasure that can emerge from liberating your hang-ups. When you let go of your hang-ups, you are truly free to be yourself!

Chapter 8: Exercises During Tantric Sex

Thus far, we have focused on the various factors that make tantric sex the best sexual experience of your life. It may seem like a big claim to make. But when you really think about it, all the time and effort you have put into learning about tantra makes it truly possible.

That is why this section is devoted to specific exercises that you can use to help you achieve the heights of sexual pleasure and ecstasy you seek to achieve. As we have mentioned throughout this book, ecstasy isn't something that happens automatically. There is a certain number of elements that go into sex before you can truly hit the heights you seek.

In this chapter, we are going to focus on exercises that you can both do solo and with your partner. Ultimately, these exercises are meant to help you stimulate your own sexual energy and that of your partner. In the end, you will find these exercises to be quite simple and very enjoyable.

Going solo

First of all, let's take a look at exercises you can do solo. These exercises are great when you don't have a partner. They are also very effective when you do have a partner. The key thing about solo exercises is that you are on your own meaning that there is no pressure to perform for anyone else. These are exercises which are yours and yours alone. So, there is no going wrong. If you find that you're not quite getting what you want out of it, then keep trying. In fact, you may find these exercises worth trying on your partner later on. It could even make for a nice surprise.

When going solo, the end game isn't always masturbation. Most people have the false assumption that anything that involves touching yourself, in any way, is about masturbation. However, this could not be farther from the truth. The exercises we are going to reveal are about self-exploration. They are about getting yourself in the right condition so that you can channel your sexual energy in a positive and meaningful manner.

Solo exercise #1: Meditation

Yes, meditation. While this isn't traditionally considered to be a "sexual" exercise, it is a must if you are really focused on mastering tantra.

In this exercise, you are focusing your mind on your energy, your sensations, and the overall arousal you feel. This will help you to explore the emotions and sensations you feel during arousal. Moreover, you can use your mind's eye to help you picture the outcome you want in a sexual relationship.

Here is a great exercise you can put into practice right away:

Find a comfortable position. This could be lying on your back in your bed or perhaps on a comfy sofa—the more comfortable the position, the better. Now, begin the exercise by breathing slowly. Inhale and exhale to the full capacity of your lungs. As you fill your lungs, picture the air entering your body. Once your lungs are full, hold your breath for about 3 seconds and then exhale. Repeat this breathing exercise as many times as you like. Don't keep count as that will only serve to distract you.

Next, picture your energy flowing through your body. Picture your sexual energy building up and coursing through every fiber of your body. If you feel slightly aroused, that's perfectly normal. Try to focus on your breathing and your energy. As you feel the energy flowing, imagine how it feeds your body. Picture how it is nourishing your cells.

Try to hold this state for as long as you can. At first, this state may only last a few minutes. As you gain more practice, you might find yourself in this position for quite a long time. Don't worry if you happen to fall asleep. Sometimes, you might be tired and stressed out. So, this type of exercise gives you a profound state of relaxation, thereby causing you to fall asleep.

Solo exercise #2: Self-massaging

Self-massaging is about exploring your own body. It's about understanding every part of your body, and in particular, the areas of your body that are most susceptible to arousal. While everyone can be aroused by touching the same areas (such as the genitals), it is also true that different folks find different parts of their bodies susceptible to pleasure. That is why this exercise is about exploring your own body. After all, if you don't know what feels good, how can you expect your partner to figure it out? Sure, they will eventually, but you can shorten the learning curve by guiding your partner.

In this exercise, start out by relaxing in a comfortable position. You can undress if you like, wear a bathrobe, or perhaps stay in your underwear. The idea is to find whatever makes your most comfortable. Then, begin by breathing just like in the previous exercise. As you relax, start by touching yourself slowly and softly. Try to get a feeling for every part of your body. Don't hold back.

As you make your way around your body, try to take in the sensations produced. You may be surprised to find that some parts are more sensitive to others. Make a note of which areas are more sensitive. Try to focus on how everything feels. If you find yourself having erotic thoughts, try your best to steer your mind back to what you are actually feeling.

One great addition to this exercise is the use of oils and lotions. These can help make your touching smoother while adding a pleasant scent. Play music if you like or use other scents such as essential oils, incense, and so on. However, try to refrain from any visual stimulation as the idea is to help you see with your other senses and not just your eyes.

Solo exercise #3: Masturbation

The intention of this exercise is not to just get off. It's about exploring pleasure and what makes you feel truly satisfied. As such, rushing orgasm is not the best way to go about it. In this exercise, the main focus is to take your time to explore your genitals and all those sensitive areas of your body.

Don't hold back!

Remember, you are alone. So, there is no one judging what you are doing. This can give you the freedom to explore all areas of your body. The worst that can happen is you find something you don't really like. Nevertheless, it's worth exploring every inch of your body.

You can set the mood just like the previous two exercises. In fact, you can do these exercises in sequence. First, start off with some meditation, then some self-massaging before masturbation. Please bear in mind that the ultimate goal is not orgasm. The ultimate goal is to manage your sensations so that you can control your arousal.

This is especially important in men. By going slow and managing your arousal, men can get more control over ejaculation, thereby prolonging the time of intercourse. As for women, this is a perfect opportunity to find what type of stimulation works best in pursuit of the big "O." Oh, and by the way, use toys if you wish!

Working with a partner

These exercises are intended to help you and your partner find the right combination of stimulation, intimacy, pleasure, and arousal. While that may sound like a great deal of things in one package, the truth is that all of these elements interact together in a single cycle. So, when you hit one target, that activates the next and so on.

So, here are three great exercises you can try with your partner:

Team exercise #1: Foreplay

There is a lot about foreplay in sexual literature. In fact, we have talked extensively about foreplay in this book. However, we haven't honed in on a couple of aspects that are essential to tantric sex.

Please bear in mind that foreplay is essential. It can be as long or as short as you like. There might be times when both of you are ready to go, while there may be others when a little more warming up is needed.

For this exercise, you can choose to undress, dress, wear costumes, lingerie, whatever hits the spot for you. Also, you can lie in bed, sit on a sofa, stand in the kitchen, be in the car (somewhere that isn't too public), or anywhere you can find the privacy and intimacy that you seek.

First, by syncing your breathing. You can use the same breathing technique we presented in solo exercise one. Now, take the time to look at each other. Explore each other's bodies with your eyes. Try to take in every aspect of your partner's body. Then, begin by touching. You can use lotion or oil if you wish. This isn't just a massage; it's touching that's meant to arouse you. As the energy builds, you can take turns touching each other, especially in those areas where you feel most sensitive. Don't forget to kiss your partner as much as you like.

At this point, you can take things to the next level. Here, you can make use of toys, or perhaps oral stimulation. If you choose, you can take turns stimulating one another. Or, you might choose to stimulate each other at the same time. Anything goes!

Please bear in mind that the point of this exercise is not sex per se. The point is to build arousal and intimacy in such a way that both of you learn what truly turns you on. In fact, you may choose to avoid sexual intercourse and perhaps bring about orgasm through the use of toys, fingers, oral, and manual stimulation. The fact is that there is nothing carved in stone. If you wish, you can have sex and make it the full package.

Team exercise #2: Snuggling or cuddling

Earlier, we described this exercise as a means of fostering intimacy. In this variation, we are going to spice things up so that it can be used as foreplay, or just as a means of stimulating arousal.

To carry out this position, we are going to be "spooning." This is a position in which both partners lie on their sides. Then, the partner that is behind the other holds the other. This creates a "giver" and "receiver."

With this exercise, you can take it as far as you like. You can lie there breathing in sync or take it up a notch. For instance, you can undress and touch. The giver takes the time to explore the receiver thereby arousing and stimulating them. If this leads to sex, then the "spoon" position is there for your enjoyment. Or, you may choose to engage in or oral or manual stimulation. Please bear in mind that this exercise isn't intended to lead to sex. It's about getting you to feel comfortable with each other's bodies so that sex becomes that much more potent.

Team exercise #3: Sex

Traditional sex is defined as intercourse, that is, penetration of some kind. Well, this isn't traditional sex. In this exercise, "sex" is anything you want it to be. In fact, you can even mix things up. Some couples feel the need for penetration every time they have sex. Other couples use penetration as the final act following the exercises outlined in this chapter. Other couples use penetration as a lead into other events such as oral or manual stimulation. And then, there are toys...

After you have truly become comfortable with your partner, sex becomes a natural occurrence that stems from stimulation and arousal. In fact, you don't really think about "sex" when you are with your partner. All you think about is enjoying your time with them. Then, things can go any way you want them, too. The main thing is to be on the same page and enjoy your encounter.

That is the bottom line. Whatever you choose to do at this point, please bear in mind that giving is just as good as receiving. So, if you feel compelled to take turns, then so be it. If you feel compelled to reach the big "O" together, then you can take your time to work yourselves up to that point.

Chapter 9: Positions During Tantric Sex

Much is written about positions in tantric sex. However, most of what you will find is a collection of various positions that don't really espouse the philosophy of tantric sex. Sure, it might be fun to try a different configuration. But at the end of the day, if your head is not into the tantric frame of mind, then the positions you try will not lead you to the ultimate ecstasy you are seeking.

With that in mind, this chapter is about taking sex positions that are a staple of tantric sex so that you can incorporate them into your own sex life right away. Sure, you may have tried them before, it's a guarantee that you haven't tried them like this before.

So, try to keep an open mind in this chapter. Now, you may not be surprised by these positions, but when you see the spin that we have put on them, you will regret no having tried this sooner!

Going on the power play

This might sound like you're playing hockey, but the power play is all about that, "power."

In this position, we're not really talking about intertwining your bodies in one manner or the other. It's about giving your partner free rein to do what they like with you. By surrendering your power, you allow your partner to take you to places you may not have been to before.

But first a disclaimer: when trying out the power play, it's important to talk about boundaries. For instance, you might say that anything in the backdoor is off-limits. Also, make a point of telling your partner what you like best. By the same token, pay attention to what drives your partner crazy. It could be that you already know how to push all of the right buttons.

That being said, the power play isn't anything like BDSM (unless you're actually into it). This is more about letting go. For instance, the use of blindfolds or masks is highly useful. The idea is that when you cancel out senses, you force the others to make up for it. Thus, your heightened sensitivity makes you feel pleasure in a whole new level.

Here is a simple yet effective angle on the powerplay.

Let's assume you are giving pleasure. Lay your partner down on their back. Use a blindfold, sleeping mask, or any other means of blocking their sight. Now, slowly undress your partner. Do it in such a way that they can anticipate your movements. The only rule is that they can't move or push you away. If you feel inclined to use handcuffs or any other type of restraint, then by all means. Now, as you approach the genital area, slowly caress their inner thigh.

At this point, you have two options. One, you can continue the caressing and proceed to masturbate your partner. In the case of a man, slowly stroking the penis will not only cause a great deal of pleasure but will allow him to control his need to ejaculate. Use lubrication if you like. In the case of a woman, stimulating the clitoris can be a great way to get things rolling. You can then choose to take your partner all the way to orgasm, or perhaps use this exercise as a warm-up.

The second option is to perform oral pleasure on your partner. The same rules apply here. You can work your way slowly so that the sensation is that much stronger. You can take your partner all the way to orgasm, or just use it as a means of setting the stage.

One of the great things about this technique is that you can use it as a means of controlling orgasm. For men, it's a great way to help control the urge to ejaculate. The trick is to get close to the "point of no return" before settling back down again. In the case of women, building up "pressure" so to speak, can lead to a massive "O." Other women may feel inclined to just have multiple orgasms as a result of oral or manual stimulation, or both.

Also, the use of toys is perfectly fine here. Just make sure that you are on the same page about the toys to be used and how they are meant to be used.

Take things slow

Throughout this book, we have talked about the importance of going slow. This is very important when you are starting out with tantra. Please bear in mind that this isn't about how hard and fast you can go. If anything, tantra is about taking things slow and relishing every moment with your partner.

At first, it's a great idea to start out with traditional positions such as the missionary and the cowgirl (or reverse if you like). With the missionary, the male is on top of the female. Now, it's important to resist the urge to go fast. Rather, the goal here is to go slow. Ideally, slow, deep penetration works really well.

Here's a simple way of ensuring this position works wonders.

Count to 4. Yes, that's right. Start out with three shorter, shallower thrusts and one deep, hard thrust. The fourth thrust should last just a little bit longer than the first three. This technique will allow you to get into a rhythm. Please bear in mind that tantra is all about finding a rhythm. When you get into that rhythm, then the female can experience a rather predictable outcome: a big "O."

In the case of the cowgirl (or reverse cowgirl), the female is on top. As such, the female is in control of the movement. So, it's a great idea to play the same 4-count: three shallow thrusts and one deep, prolonged thrust. This will allow the female to control the sensation thereby enabling a rhythmic movement.

You will find that even though these are very traditional positions, they really work very well when you are able to build a rhythm. Eventually, both of you will be able to sync everything, movement, breathing, and eye contact. If you choose to cancel sight, then breathing becomes highly important in order to ensure you are on the same page.

The final lap

This is the classic tantric sex position. In this one, the man sits upright, preferably with his back up against something firm for support, legs stretched out (not crossed). Then, the woman sits on his lap. The woman's legs should wrap around the man's buttocks. Kneeling is not recommended as it can get quite tiring very quickly. She can then wrap her arms around the man's neck or use her hands to caress him. The man can also wrap his arms around the woman or use his hands to caress her.

This is a very intimate position as it always for a number of things. First, kissing is the go-to option here. Also, it's great for breathing exercises. You can simply hold each other and attempt to sync your breathing. In addition, you can caress each other in unison. For instance, massaging each other's backs, buttocks and chest are all good exercises.

The other great thing about this position is that you can achieve penetration with it. So, if you want to take it up a notch, then it's certainly an option. One interesting thing about this position is that due to its nature, you can't move very fast. So, it's ideal for tantra. Plus, the level of intimacy you can achieve with this position is excellent.

The reverse lap

This position is essentially the same as the previous with a twist: one of the partners sits with their back to the wall while the other sits on their lap but with their back facing their partner. As such, the first partner only sees the back of the second. The second partner is essentially the recipient of the former's attention.

When engaging in this position, the first partner essentially has access to the second partner. They can caress just about every part of their partner's body while having the option of kissing the back of their neck, shoulders, and upper back.

One of the great things about this position is that you can switch things up. So, the man can hold the female, or the female can hold the male. So, it's great for taking turns and pampering each other. If you choose to penetrate, the female can sit on the man's lap and do so. At this point, the position works pretty much like a reverse cowgirl. And just like the previous position, there's not much room to move fast. So, you really don't have much choice but to take it slow.

One very nice variation of this position is that it can be done in a bathtub, jacuzzi, or a swimming pool. If you're in public, well, you have to keep it civil. But in private, you can take it up as far as you want to. A bubble bath is one of the go-to moves for this position.

Spooning

Earlier, we talked about how spooning can be a great tool for fostering intimacy. In this case, it's also a great position for having intercourse. Additionally, it works really well because you can't move very fast even if you wanted to. Spooning can work both ways as the female can hold the male and vice-versa. If you are intent on penetration, then it works very well, especially because it favors syncing your movements. Plus, it's one of the most intimate positions you will find in the tantric sex toolkit.

The other great thing about spooning is that it can be quite erotic without necessarily leading to sex. It's good for syncing breathing and it's also good for post-sex cuddling. In fact, lots of couples love sleeping like this. So, that's an added bonus.

One other twist to spooning is the ability to masturbate your partner. This works well if you're keen on pleasuring your partner. In fact, you can practice syncing up your breathing while masturbating your partner. As you can see, it's the position that keeps on giving!

Mutual masturbation

On the subject of touching, mutual masturbation is a great way of syncing everything up. This technique works well to sync breathing, practice eye contact, and also kissing passionately. So, let's take a look at a couple of ways in which you could make this work.

The first is by both partners lying on their backs. Then touching ensues. But the key here is that the touching needs to be at the same speed. If one goes faster than the other, you might get a big "O" ahead of time. Also, it might be a bit hard to focus when your partner is going at a different rate than you are.

Another position is lying on your side, facing one another. This position allows you to make eye contact, kiss, and basically have access to the entire front part of your partner's body. This variation is great if you are just looking to lie in bed, spend some time together, and throw in a fun ending.

The third variation to sit, facing each other. For this one, both partners sit upright on the same surface. So, one does not sit on the lap of the other. This variation is great for eye contact and breathing. It also allows you both to touch each other slowly. Given the nature of the position, you can't go very fast. That is a great thing in the world of tantra, of course.

So, there you have some great position which you can practice today. Please keep in mind that anything goes in tantra. You can do any of the positions you enjoy. However, the ones we have presented in this chapter are intended to help you get into the rhythm of tantra. Eventually, you'll be able to mix things up as suits your mood.

Chapter 10: Massages During Tantric Sex

Massaging has to be the most recognizable part of tantric sex. All experts on the topic recommend the use of massaging as a means of engaging in tantra. However, not too many experts take the time to explain while massaging is such a useful tactic when it comes to tantric sex.

The main reason behind massaging's effectiveness is that it promotes a sensory response that other techniques don't really provide. This is important as tantra is based, first and foremost, on sensory perception. After all, traditional sex is "traditional" because it's just about finding the quickest way to orgasm.

When you take the time to practice massage, you will discover a two-way street that you had no idea already existed. First, the incredible sensation that comes with receiving a tantric massage. The second, the unbelievable satisfaction that comes with giving your partner a tremendous experience. Both of these situations can leave you feeling both satisfied and nurtured.

Massaging roles

Basically, there are two roles in tantric massaging, the giver and receiver. The giver is the person performing the massage while the receiver is the one who is the recipient of the massage. Both roles are important in tantra as each partner connects to the other, thus producing the tantric experience.

If you are more inclined to a dominant or submissive role, massaging provides a great opportunity to feed this side. For example, more dominant individuals can take their partners into their hands, literally, and give them an extraordinary experience. If you are a more submissive person, then you can fully surrender yourself in your partner's touch.

However, massaging is also great at inverting the power dynamic. More predominantly submissive individuals can take the opportunity to be in the lead. They can give their dominant partner some much-deserved attention and pampering. The dominant partner has the chance to relinquish power for a short while. This can be a refreshing change that can help a dominant individual get away from their comfort zone to find a different role in the relationship.

Massaging also allows each partner to take turns. It's a bit hard to massage each other at the same time. So, the best way to go about it is to just take turns. Now, it can be hard to receive a massage, pop up, and then give one. As such, you might work out a deal in which one receives a massage on one occasion and then the other on the next occasion.

Still, taking turns can work well if you plan on simpler things like a shoulder rub or foot massage (this is awesome if you have a foot fetish). So, do make time for massaging as part of your love life. If you haven't given it a try, you'll regret not having done it sooner.

Setting the stage

Setting the stage for a massage is highly important. If you are keen on pulling out all the stops, a massage table is the best way to go. Alternatively, just lying in bed is great. Lying on a couch also works, but because of the design of couches, it can be a bit tough to access all of your partner's body.

Scented candles, essential oils, or incense are great ways of providing a pleasant smell. Soft music, nature sounds, or some smooth jazz can also enhance the mood. Visuals are important too, such as dim lighting or perhaps candlelight.

One very important aspect of setting the stage is to minimize distractions. This means blocking out the world around you. Please keep in mind that both the giver and receiver ought to focus on the events as they are happening. So, eliminating distractions is a must.

An interesting twist could be to massage your partner in a tub or jacuzzi. You can make use of bath salts to create a pleasant atmosphere. This works exceptionally well when you are looking to alleviate stress. Water has a great way of making aches and pains go away. Plus, massages in water tend to be a lot more intimate than say in bed or massage table.

Using equipment

This largely depends on what you are going for. You can keep things very simple by just using your hands and some oil. There are various types of oil that you can use on your partner. The most common type of oil is regular baby oil. It serves as a very nice lubricant while also stimulating the skin. There is also a wide range of massage oils. Some are scented while others vary in texture. So, it's up to you to experiment with whatever you feel would work best for you.

Additionally, if you are inclined to use any sex toys, feel free to bring them into the mix (more on that in a minute). Any other props such as mallets, rubber balls, or vibrators could enhance the experience. In a way, massaging is about trial and error. This means that you can try out various things and see what works best for you. If you find that one thing doesn't work, then you can just move on from it.

A good piece of advice here is to avoid rushing out to buy a bunch of massage gear. Start out with your hands and move on from there. The best equipment which you can use is your hands!

The proper technique

When using tantric massage, the question of the "proper technique" comes to mind. Often, folks are unsure about whether to rub, or stroke, or do karate chops. The fact of the matter is that you don't need to be a professional massage therapist to give your partner a pleasurable experience. In fact, you can just start out by running your hands down your partner's limbs, back, and shoulder. In addition, the use of oils can greatly reduce the amount of friction when rubbing your partner down. So, that creates the warm sensation of being touched while also allowing yourself to control the movements you are doing.

One interesting spin is to take a couple's massage class. In this type of class, a trained professional shows you how to rub down your partner. So, it's not them doing the rubbing; it's you, but with the guidance of a pro. For couples looking to build an intimate experience, this class actually works really well despite having a third person in the room with you.

Alternatively, online tutorials can help you get a good sense of what to do and how to handle your partner. In fact, watching such tutorials can even create arousal. In a manner of speaking, it provides a great visual.

With that in mind, here is a great four-step plan you can put into practice right away.

First, let's start with relaxation. To get ready for a massage, you can practice breathing with your partner. The receiver lies down on their back while the giver sets the pace for breathing. The giver can begin by providing light caresses on the legs, arms, or just simply being there.

Next, as relaxation sets in, work your way up. To do this, begin by providing a foot rub, working your way up on the calves, shins, and thighs. You don't need any particular technique here. Basically, all you need is light rubbing with your hands or the oil of your choice. Lotion works well, too.

After, try to avoid the genital area at this point. While you might be tempted to go for it, it's best to wait until you have completed the entire body massage. While you might have a happy ending for your partner in mind, the main point of the tantric massage is to foster intimacy and give your partner the best experience. As such, you can caress their inner thigh, eventually working your way up their stomach, chest, and down their arms.

Once you have reached the shoulders, ask your partner to flip over on to their belly. Now, you can work your way down their back to their buttocks and the back of their legs. At this point, you can focus on their thighs. Here, you can decide to stimulate the genital area if you wish. You can ask your partner to flip back on to their back to focus on their genital area.

Lastly, it's important to be aware of what the point of the massage is. If you want to use the massage as a means of foreplay prior to sexual intercourse, then certainly stimulating your partner's genital area serves the purpose. You can use your hands or even perform oral pleasure. The use of toys can also work here.

If the point of the massage is not sexual per se, then you can leave it at that. Please bear in mind that if you are not planning on any sexual activity as it relates to the massage, then make this clear to your partner, so there are no expectations. However, the chances are that you may not resist and choose to take it further.

Happy ending?

This question always comes up when discussing tantric massages. In general, you can provide your partner with a happy ending if you are both comfortable with it. This is important to note, as you may not be comfortable with this idea at first. Generally speaking, the giver may feel left out if the receiver orgasms while they don't receive any reciprocal pleasure.

One of the deals you can make it to take turns. You can choose to pamper your partner one day while you are in line for the next round. Otherwise, you could take turns massaging one another before sexual activity.

The fact of the matter is that massages provide you with the opportunity to foster both intimacy and to pamper your partner. Please bear in mind that one of the core tenets is to provide your partner with the attention they seek. By the same token, you should also be on the receiving end. This is why we have stated throughout this book that tantra is a two-way street. Of course, communication is the key in this regard.

What to watch out for

While tantric massages are more about providing your partner with an experience that goes beyond the actual massage technique you are using, it's worth mentioning that you and your partner should communicate on what feels good and what you enjoy most. For instance, you might have highly sensitive areas. As such, your partner needs to be aware of this. Likewise, you need to be aware of which areas are sensitive to your partner.

Also, setting a time and place for massages is key. While that may sound mechanical (like having to set an appointment) the fact is that improvising a massage session may not provide you with the results you seek. This is why many tantra practitioners make time for themselves and their partners. Since you want to dedicate as much time and attention as you can to the occasion, making time for your partner is a must.

On the whole, tantric massage is a technique that evolves among partners. Over time, you will find what works for both of you. Then, you can take that knowledge and translate it into an experience which makes sense for both you. That way, your massage sessions will become as pleasurable as they can become. If this leads to sex, then so be it. If it doesn't lead to sex, then it's still a wonderful experience that can set the stage for further sessions.

Please keep in mind that tantra isn't necessarily about sex. This misconception tends to permeate the minds of folks all over. When you see that tantra is just the overarching theme that also happens to include sex, you will find that your overall feelings about your sex life and your relationship with your partner change drastically.

So, make the time for yourself and your partner. You won't regret prioritizing this part of your life.

Chapter 11: What is Tantric Pleasure?

Pleasure is the most talked-about aspect regarding tantra. After all, what point would there be to tantra is there wasn't any pleasure involved?

The fact of the matter is pleasure is the core of the entire tantra practice. Pleasure is of the utmost importance. So, that's why we are going to have an in-depth discussion on pleasure and what it means to give it and receive it.

As we have stated numerous times in this book, tantra is a two-way street. As such, tantra is both about giving and receiving. Unlike other approaches in which students are taught to either give or receive pleasure, tantra is about reciprocity. This means that you should get as much as you give and vice-versa. If you feel that you are giving more than you get, then something is not entirely right. Good tantra practice means that you are able to feel as satisfied as your partner.

What is tantric pleasure?

Now, the question begs: what is pleasure?

Generally speaking, pleasure is a feeling of goodness in your physical body. This feeling is the result of engaging in a pleasurable sexual activity. The degree of pleasure that you are able to feel depends on your partner, the activities you do, and your ability to actually feel pleasure.

This is important as there are many folks out there who have trouble feeling pleasure. A common issue with feeling pleasure is generally associated with the feelings you might have about the activities in which you are engaging. For some, sex is synonymous with impure activities. For others, they may feel guilty about feeling pleasure.

While it is not our intention to explore the causes of being unable to feel pleasure, we are looking to establish that pleasure is about feeling good when engaging in sexual activity. Pleasure derived from traditional sex is limited to the physical body. This means that you are able to feel pleasure though it doesn't go beyond a temporary feeling of satisfaction.

For men, pleasure is generally derived from penetration or oral stimulation. For women, pleasure is also derived from penetration or oral stimulation though it should be noted that there is an emotional component that also provides pleasure.

In addition, sensory experience also produces pleasure. Visual stimulation is key while olfactory and auditory stimulation also plays a key role. On the whole, you should strive to combine as many senses as possible during sexual encounters. This will enhance the overall feeling of pleasure derived from the sexual act itself.

Yet, we haven't defined "tantric pleasure."

Tantric pleasure is the result of feeling pleasure at a physical, emotional, and even spiritual level. This type of pleasure is the result of your ability to connect on a deep level with your partner. As such, you are not merely finding physical gratification. You are entering a realm of profound connection that goes beyond the mere physical encounter.

When you hit this level, you are not only satisfying the physical, instinctive desire, but you are also nourishing your spiritual and emotional need for connection. When you really think about it, this is why many folks say they are left with an empty feeling after sex.

What's the reason?

The lack of emotional connection with their partner!

Now, you could develop a strong, emotional connection with someone you've just met. This can happen simply based on the fact that you have an open mind. In other words, you are open to communicating with someone on a deeper level. While this isn't something that happens with everyone you meet, it is something that can certainly happen when you know what you are looking for.

All about physical pleasure

The first step to tantric pleasure is physical. This is the starting point. As such, we can't ignore this point. In fact, if you try to skip physical pleasure and go straight to an emotional connection, you are missing a very important component.

Physical pleasure is vital as this is what fosters the overall enjoyment of the sexual encounter. Even though it's true that you can have a tantric experience without sexual intercourse, there is still a strong physical component. For example, when you have a tantric massage, there is a strong physical connection. Just the fact that you are doing the massage is enough to get you to really feel good at a physical level.

Also, physical pleasure is vital is generating the positive energies that course through your body. Without it, it would be very hard to achieve a sense of wellness. The key here is that there is a clear mind-body-spirit connection. So, you cannot ignore the physical. It is important and must be given its proper place.

Another important aspect of physical pleasure is the sensory experience that goes with a tantric session. You see, we perceive the world around us through our senses. As such, we can't expect to have a full tantric experience without being cognizant of the role our senses play. In this regard, setting the scene is pivotal in ensuring that you, and your partner, get the most out of your experience.

Establishing an emotional connection

As far as emotional connections go, it's not always easy to develop one. If you have ever been with a person in which your relationship did not involve any kind of feelings, then you can appreciate how empty this type of relationship can be. When you are devoid of emotional connections, you can't fully appreciate the level of passion between two people.

That is why tantra focuses heavily on developing intimacy. As we have stated on several occasions, tantra is not necessarily about sex. It's about creating an emotional connection through intimacy, which can bring you and your partner together. When you make a point of executing the exercises we have presented, you can build intimacy with your partner at a very deep level.

Please bear in mind that intimacy is built on trust. When you build trust, you can create a feeling in which you are certain that every encounter with your partner will be a memorable one. Even if there is no sex involved, you can be sure that it will make your life that much more enjoyable.

Emotional connections are also built outside of the bedroom. The overall tantric experience can carry over into your everyday life. If you are in a committed relationship, you can see how the small things truly add up. For instance, showing genuine concern for your partner breeds the type of trust that cannot be easily matched. In addition, your attention and devotion to your partner will signify how much they mean to you.

Does that mean you need to spend every waking moment with them?

Of course not.

But it does mean that the time you devote to them must count. There is no point in spending time with them for the sake of spending time, as this will not foster the type of relationship you are looking to build. That is why your dedication to building intimacy is crucial when it comes to tantra.

Here is an important reflection on intimacy: intimacy is a hard thing to build. It generally takes a long time to build, but it can be easily destroyed. Your actions can quickly undermine the intimacy you have worked hard to build. This is why it's always recommended that you, and your partner, take the time to work out any unresolved issues between you. Such issues create a wedge in between you. So, it's best to get them out of the way so that there is nothing lurking in the shadows.

Building a spiritual connection

Once you have built a strong physical connection and a deep emotional bond, you can then move on to building a spiritual connection. This connection is not easily attained. It is generally the result of trust and understanding. That is why you can't expect to skip a physical and emotional connection in order to get to a spiritual connection.

However, there is a "chicken or the egg" dilemma that arises when considering spiritual connections. Does the spiritual connection happen first, and that leads to a physical connection, or does the physical connection happen first, and that leads to the spiritual connection?

This dilemma can be answered in the following manner:

It depends on the circumstances.

There are times when two people have an instant physical attraction. This is commonly called "chemistry." So, when you see two people have chemistry, they quickly develop a strong physical bond. This bond may be expanded to include an emotional component. For instance, a purely physical relationship can develop into a romance. This romantic nature is when people "fall in love." Thus, it should be noted that falling in love is a question of a deep emotional bond that cannot be cast aside. Then, the relationship may evolve into a deeper spiritual connection. This is commonly seen in those couples who claim to know what their partner is thinking. Such relationships are rare but do provide an interesting point of view on going from a physical to a spiritual connection.

The flip side of this question is when two people are drawn to each other for some mysterious reason. This can be seen in the way "opposites attract," or someone has that "X factor." When you see these relationships, there is a deeper bond that cannot be easily ignored. The spiritual bond can then evolve into a deeper emotional and then physical connection. The end result is a platonic relationship that morphs into a physical one.

In either of these cases, there is a logical process in which the two parties move through a natural progression. It's not the type of thing in which you are hitting things off one day, and then deeply in love the next. Also, you can't expect to admire someone for immaterial reasons and then jump in the sack with them. There has to be a natural progression through the various stages of a deep and meaningful relationship. Granted, there are times when things happen very quickly. However, it's not the type of thing that can happen overnight.

Using tantra as a means of deepening connections

Can tantra be used to help a couple progress through the various stages of a relationship?

We thought you'd never ask!

Tantra is perfect for helping couples go from one stage of their relationship with another. In particular, tantra can help those couples that have been in a relationship for a while but seem to have lost that spark. As such, it's a great way or rekindling that passion that may have been lost over the years. As a matter of fact, tantra has been known to help couples rediscover each other in ways that they may have forgotten. If this sounds like you, then you must try tantra right away.

In the event that you are in a new relationship, tantra can help you settle into a dynamic in which you can go about discovering everything about one another. It can help you set the tone for your relationship moving forward. As a matter of fact, it's a great way of bonding especially if you've had negative experiences in the past. Tantra can deepen the bond between you while also helping you find a balance between the physical and the spiritual.

If you are single, then take this opportunity to wrap your mind around the tantra philosophy. You will find that being alone gives you a good opportunity to assess the situation you are in and make any changes you see fit moving forward. That will enable you to become the best version of yourself. That way, when you are ready to be in a relationship, you can make the most of your time with your new partner.

What could be better than that?

Chapter 12: The Male Orgasm

In a nutshell, the male orgasm is commonly associated with ejaculation. There would be no need to write any more about it if we kept this narrow perspective. However, when we take a broader perspective on this subject, we can see that orgasm and ejaculation are two completely different concepts. Yes, they are linked; however, they are not mutually bound to one another. This implies that men can have orgasms, multiple orgasms even, without the need to ejaculate.

If this is something that surprises you, then you might be surprised to find that an orgasm is not necessarily a physiological response to sexual arousal. Rather, it is an electrochemical reaction in the brain, which triggers the sensation of pleasure.

How does this work?

In order to fully understand how the male orgasm works, it's important to understand the entire dynamic that goes on within the male body and how this pertains to the ultimate climax of pleasure.

How arousal works

Men are predominantly visual creatures. This is the direct result of evolution. The male brain evolved in accordance with the needs and the environment in which early humans developed. Since the traditional male role was that of hunter-gatherer, the male brain developed a much broader set of skills related to vision. Consequently, males are much more inclined toward visuals rather than other senses, such as hearing.

Over the centuries, this visual nature has not diminished. Men are still predominantly visual. This is why many of the typically male professions deal with the measurement of distance and space in addition to calculations of speed, volume, mass, and so on. While this doesn't mean that women cannot do these professions, men are more biologically suited for them.

That being said, arousal in males is typically a visual event. Therefore, males are far more attracted to a visually esthetic female than females would be to a visually attractive male. As such, males tend to focus on a certain set of features that are considered to be attractive. For example, males find a youthful look much more appealing as it signals an instinctive reaction indicating that the female is apt for procreation.

When attraction, at a physical level, takes place, the brain signals the body to start moving blood flow to the genital area. To do this, the heart needs to work a little bit harder to ensure that blood flow is sufficient. In addition, the heart works harder, but blood vessels also need to widen in order to accommodate the increased blood flow. This is what eventually leads to an erection.

Now, let's assume that sex is about to take place. While arousal is happening, there is no sensation of pleasure yet. After all, if there is no "action," then there cannot be any presence of pleasure. This is where traditional sex gets it wrong.

In traditional sexual culture, men are taught to stimulate their genital area in such a way that pleasurable sensations are sent throughout the body; the brain decodes it and floods the body with feel-good chemicals such as endorphins. However, when the arousal stage moves into actual sex, if there is no control over the psychological aspects of the event, then what you end up having is the male ejaculating. This reaction is often confused with orgasm. Yet, it is a known fact that ejaculation and orgasm are two separate phenomena.

Why?

You see, ejaculation is a physiological response that is associated with procreation. Naturally, this function has to feel good. Otherwise, why would humans procreate if sex was unpleasant? Mother nature needed to make sure that it felt good so that the species could reproduce and thrive.

With that in mind, arousal leads to orgasm when a male is able to separate ejaculation from pleasure. When a male is engaged in tantric sex, his focus is moved away from the various aspects of sexual relations to the more emotional and even spiritual aspects of it. As such, his focus is moved away from feeling good physically, to enjoying the overall experience of it.

Many tantra practitioners say that they feel a greater sense of arousal and stimulation by letting go of their physiological sensations and focusing more on the sensory experience. This includes breathing and touching. Also, very powerful emotions are unleashed when males are able to focus on their partner's pleasure in addition to their own.

Getting to the big "O."

At this point, the big "O" becomes a question of the brain being able to process the sensory perception in such a way that it releases massive amounts of endorphins (among other substances) into the bloodstream. There is a cocktail of brain chemicals such as adrenaline and serotonin. The interaction of the chemicals in the brain leads to the overall feeling of pleasure. However, the interaction of these chemicals leads to overloading the nervous system to the point where an incredible sensation of pleasure takes over the entire nervous system in a wave-like manner.

This is an orgasm.

Guys who feel these orgasms during sex report they feel their erections getting stronger without the need to ejaculate. While the pleasure signals are there, they are not directly linked to the overall feeling of needing to ejaculate.

This is how you can separate one thing from the other.

In theory, this sounds all well and fine. But being able to achieve it is an entirely different ballgame. The challenge here is to overcome the conditioning instilled during adolescence. In many cases, adolescent boys learn that "faster is better." Sadly, this is a tremendous disservice that is done to mean as they grow up without being able to truly enjoy sex for what it's worth.

By fostering the erroneous perception that finishing fast is the best way, men are taught to deprive themselves of the magical experience that comes with truly enjoying sex with their chosen partner. When a man is able to achieve true orgasm, there is no comparison. This is why tantra is such a seemingly mysterious art form.

The good news here is that anyone can achieve true orgasms. Best of all, any man can achieve multiple orgasms while only needing to ejaculate once. If this sounds new to you, then do read on as we will describe the steps that you can take you to achieve this.

First, it's time to dissociate orgasm and ejaculation. They are two separate concepts. Orgasms are electrochemical reactions in the brain, while ejaculation is a physiological response to arousal and stimulation. The sooner you are able to separate these concepts from your mind, the sooner you'll be able to truly enjoy the time you spend with your partner.

Next, let go of the idea that the ultimate goal of sex is… sex. Of course, the main point of sex is to engage in intercourse with your partner. However, it is focusing solely on sex that makes it hard for a man to truly enjoy the situation. Generally, there is so much pressure to "perform." As such, this creates unneeded pressure. Why would you put so much pressure on yourself to do something pleasurable? Do you put so much pressure on yourself to eat properly? If you did, you wouldn't know a bit of anything you ate.

The same goes for sex. So, take the time to enjoy and savor all of the emotions, sights, and experiences that come with being someone you are attracted to, or even someone you love. This makes the entire experience much more rewarding.

Now, when you are in the midst of intercourse with your partner, try your best to remove your mind from what you are doing. This sounds paradoxical but the fact that is that if you concentrate on "doing it," then you end up getting caught up in not finishing too soon. Plus, your mind begins to play tricks on you. You start to wonder if your partner is enjoying it or if you are doing it right. These tricks are highly detrimental to your level of satisfaction while limiting the amount of enjoyment the both of you can derive from an encounter.

This is why tantra is about slowing the pace of the game. When you slow the pace of the game, you have the option to exert more control over the situation. If you feel that you are about to lose control, you can slow things down or even stop altogether. Some men find it useful to pull out and focus on touching, kissing, and caressing their partner while things settle down. Again, if your goal is to give your partner an orgasm, then you only see half of the picture. But if your goal is to give your partner the best possible experience, then you are on the right track.

Lastly, use your mind to focus your energy. This means that you ought to use your mind to move your energy throughout your body. Imagine your energy flowing throughout your body, nourishing everything in its path. This energy not only serves as a means of charging the body, but it also serves as a means of helping your body heal and repair itself. That might seem a bit strange. However, sex is known to promote healing energy within the body.

Additionally, you can recycle that energy between you and your partner. This is an energy that you are both sharing as a result of the mutual pleasure that you are sharing. When you both take the time to really savor your encounter, you will find that the "pressure" builds up. As this pressure builds up, the release of energy is an amazing feeling, unlike anything you've felt before. These are the mind-blowing orgasms that come with tantric sex.

Making sense of male pleasure

There is nothing wrong with feeling pleasure. It's a logical consequence of sex. If you believe that feeling pleasure is somehow wrong, you are only hurting yourself insofar as depriving yourself of wonderful experiences. In addition, you are also depriving your partner of having a wonderful experience alongside you.

So, finding true tantric pleasure is about framing your mind in such a way that you can enjoy the situation by taking in all the senses. Therefore, you can't rush this process. This isn't the type of process which you can complete with an egg timer. This is the type of process in which you need to be present at the moment things are happening. If your mind is wandering off, then you can't really make it work. By the same token, if your mind is focused on "performing," then the chances of you actually enjoying your encounter is far less.

Experienced tantra practitioners know that sex isn't about keeping score. There isn't some magic number that you need to hit in order to considered "good." What you will find is that there is a threshold in which you know you are moving in the right direction. This threshold is different for everyone. Nevertheless, your partner will be quite clear in showing you where they are going. If the experience is pleasurable for them, they will surely make it obvious.

So, if you are putting pressure on yourself to perform, it's time to drop those expectations and focus on sex for what it is. Take the time to assess your expectations and bring them into perspective. Your job, if you will, is to create an experience that your partner will thoroughly enjoy. This includes everything around you, from the scene, the sights, smells, sounds, and of course, sex.

Beyond that, please keep in mind that sex is a work in progress. You can't expect to hit the heights of tantric sex right away. While the guidelines we have laid out will make an immediate impact, you can't expect to hit the heights immediately. It takes time to really click with your partner. Of course, it doesn't take years, but it does take a concerted effort to make sure that you and your partner get what you want about of your sex life.

Chapter 13: The Female Orgasm

In most literature, it seems that the female orgasm is shrouded in mystery. Some so-called experts claim that it's quite easy to find multiple orgasms. They make it seems as though there is some kind of switch you can simply flip and off you go.

Other gurus make it seem like it some kind of unattainable phenomenon that can only be uncovered by the proprietary method. As such, you stand no chance of achieving orgasm unless you follow their time-tested, patented moves.

The fact of the matter is that the female orgasm works in the same way that the male orgasm does. The female orgasm is an electrochemical reaction that releases all of the chemicals that produce the wonderful feelings that come with having a good time in bed.

However, it is also important to point out that the road to the female orgasm is different. Even if the overall reaction is the same for both men and women, getting there is a bit different. This means that you need to focus on the various components that lead up to the big "O."

In this chapter, we are going to be focusing on the elements which lead up to that big "O." In particular, we're going to be discussing the main reasons why reaching orgasm can be difficult. With the ideas that we will present, you'll be able to get a much broader perspective on the limitations that you may be encountering.

Arousal in women

Unlike men, women are not predominantly visual. Yes, women find visual stimulation highly enjoyable. Women value the visual esthetics of an attractive individual as much as men do. The difference is that women do not value visual attractiveness above everything else. In fact, women tend to value visual symmetry a lot more than men do.

When talking about symmetry, it's important to keep in mind that women enjoy men who look proportionate. That is why most women don't find bodybuilders particularly attractive. The same goes for men who are too thin or those who are obese. The secret is maintaining a proportionate look in terms of height and weight. This means that while men don't need a chiseled body to be attractive, trying to maintain proper proportions makes a huge difference.

The way arousal works in women is that you have an overall sensory experience that leads to a set of emotions. It is this emotional connection between sex and emotions that leads to a pleasant sexual experience. In a manner of speaking, if your heart is not into it, then arousal can be hard to pursue.

Of course, there is instinctive arousal which is mainly driven by the need for physical intimacy. However, this need for physical intimacy is often confused with sex. Sadly, culture has reduced intimacy with sex. The reality is that sex is only one part of intimacy. This is why we have made a strong case for the need to incorporate intimacy in your life without making sex the main priority. When you take the need for sex out of the equation, you are left with the entire scene around you. When this scene isn't there, then you have no choice but to build it.

Fostering arousal should then become about creating a safe atmosphere in which you feel comfortable being yourself. Now, this is crucial as feeling uncomfortable, in any way, can be a huge detrimental factor in limiting your ability to truly enjoy sex. When you feel comfortable with yourself and everything you are doing, then you can certainly make things work as best as it can for you.

What's holding you back

Inexperienced individuals tend to relate the inability to orgasm to physiological factors. They believe that there is something physical that affects your ability to orgasm. The fact is that there are many more psychological and emotional factors that affect your ability to orgasm. That's why the exercises in this book have been presented so that you can put yourself in the proper frame of mind. When this occurs, you are able to truly make yourself feel open and liberated. When you find this sense of liberation, you can then go about enjoying yourself to the fullest.

So, what's holding you back?

The fact is that there is any number of issues which can wreak havoc on your mind at any given point. In particular, being uncomfortable with your body can play a largely detrimental role in helping you liberate yourself. You see, we tend to compare ourselves to certain standards all the time. We compared ourselves to "good" mothers, "successful" professionals, or "good-looking" people.

When it comes to you, and your physical appearance, there is no need to compare yourself to anyone else. Sure, you might be keen on improving your physical conditioning and fitness. But that doesn't mean you are not attractive. If your partner values you for who you are, then you already have the most important aspect of attractiveness. This is why it's important to let go of such hang-ups in the bedroom. Being too overly focused on this aspect will limit your ability to truly enjoy yourself.

Also, stress plays a huge factor in holding you back. When stress gets the best of you, it can be nearly impossible to shut your mind off. If anything, you'll be faced with nagging voices in your head that won't leave you alone. You might be really enjoying yourself when you are suddenly hit with a flood of thoughts regarding any number of things. These thoughts can totally undermine your ability to truly enjoy yourself.

To combat this, the breathing and relaxation techniques we have presented are highly effective. In addition, making time for yourself and your partner means that you have the freedom to enjoy yourselves without being concerned with other things. Just being able to forget about your phone for a while is enough to get you feeling completely liberated from the world around you.

Another crucial factor is to address any issues that may be driving a wedge between you and your partner. Unfortunately, all couples have issues, especially if they have been together for a while. Often, unresolved issues fester beneath the surface. So, you don't really see them superficially. But below the surface, they are clearly affecting the way you interact with your partner. As such, if there is anything that is affecting your relationship, it's important to deal with it, get it out of the way, and move on. If you let it sit there, it will gnaw at you. This will become evident as you engage in tantric practices. You might start okay, but if such thoughts should hit you, you won't be able to recover. You'll have no choice to get over it or struggle with them throughout your tantric sessions.

Getting to the big "O."

There is a general misconception that it is hard to get to the big "O." The fact is that it's neither easy nor hard. It's just a question of knowing how to go about it. This implies that when you are committed to the experience you are living, you can find the pleasure you seek. Many times, it's just a matter of getting lost in the moment. This is why we have mentioned the need to live "in the now." When you manage to get everything out of the way, you can find the path to true pleasure and ecstasy.

Unfortunately, the big "O" seems like an elusive target. This occurs when you are completely focused on getting there without really taking in the entire experience. This puts unnecessary pressure on you. After all, why make orgasms the main attraction to sex when there are so many other things happening?

This is an important consideration as sex is filled with various situations and occurrences. You have intimacy, touch, sights, scents, and also your role in giving your partner pleasure. With all of those things happening all at once, there is no reason why you should become fixated on just one.

When you let go of your pursuit of the big "O," you will find that everything becomes much more enjoyable. You won't find yourself completely focused on getting there. Rather, you will enjoy the journey, so to speak. It's a means of enjoying the read even if you don't reach the final destination. Sure, it would be great if you did, but if you don't, it wouldn't be the end of the world.

Something else to consider is that tantra allows you to build up enough experience so that you can learn exactly what buttons to push and when to push them. The various exercises that we have presented throughout this book will enable you to find the right spots for you. This means that you won't have to guess. You'll know exactly where the road will take you. Ultimately, this is a comforting situation as you won't have to doubt or second-guess yourself.

The path to the big "O."

Here is a very simple exercise which you can do to get you to the big "O" every time.

First, think about the road you will be traveling on. This could be a massage, a massage followed by sex, or perhaps just a moment of intimacy with your partner. When you visualize what you are about to do with your partner, it builds anticipation. This anticipation plays a nice erotic game with you as you become expectant of what can happen. When you build up with anticipation, you naturally become aroused. Unless you're not feeling up to it, just the sheer anticipation of a sexual encounter is enough to get your curiosity moving.

Next, see with your eyes what your partner is doing. Take in the sights, sounds, and scents of what's going. This could be a massage, cuddling, or intercourse. It really doesn't matter. The idea is to take in everything that's happening.

Then, close your eyes and try to "see" it in your mind's eye. Try to visualize everything movement, touch, or thrust. In a manner of speaking, you are translating what your body feels to what your mind can see. If you wish, you can limit your visual capabilities. For example, a blindfold or sleeping mask can work quite well.

Since your mind is occupied trying to recreate a visual from what you are feeling, you are more concentrated on taking in the sensory experience rather than actually seeing the events unfold. As you render these images in your mind, you will find that the sensory experience builds up.

After, try your best to anticipate the next move. If you are in control, say in a cowgirl position, try to anticipate your next move. In a manner of speaking, you are planning what to do next as you go. When you do this, you are building up even more anticipation. As such, you are avoiding a mechanical motion by transforming in order to into a fluid movement.

Lastly, as you feel the pressure building up, don't try to chase the big "O." Instead, picture that energy coursing through your body. Imagine how that energy can race through every fiber of your body. When you feel it rushing toward you, don't try to catch it. Just let it come to you. If you try to pursue it, you'll end up disappointing yourself as you may not end up catching up to it. In fact, orgasms can be quite elusive once you are really close. However, when you don't make a point of trying to catch it, then you'll find that it will simply come to you. And when it does, you'll know it's there. You'll be able to relish in the feeling that comes with experience full-on pleasure. In the end, you won't have anything to surpass the feeling that comes with finding yourself completely immersed in this kind of experience.

If that isn't enough for you, then don't worry. There is still more to come!

Chapter 14: Individual Ecstasy

Thus far, we have presented an extensive approach that can lead you, at your partner, to find pleasure and ecstasy. In a manner of speaking, this is about working in tandem to reach this goal. However, pleasure is an individual feeling that may, or may not, be easily achieved. It's important to take this into consideration as it's not always easy to find the bliss that you seek. If only it were as easy as turning on a faucet.

This is why experienced tantra practitioners are just as able to find pleasure themselves as they are able to help their partners find it. This becomes even more important when an experienced tantra practitioner finds a partner who is new to it. By virtue of their experience, they can help the newcomer find the heights of sexual pleasure.

In this chapter, we are going to take a look at how you can help your partner find pleasure and ecstasy, especially in those cases when it is hard for them to focus, enjoy themselves, and make the most of your experiences together.

Helping your partner find ecstasy

There are times when, for any number of reasons, your partner just isn't getting there. This could be due to something like being unable to forget about a stressful event, or perhaps having trouble reaching the big "O." This is where both of you need to keep in mind that the goal is not to find the biggest possible "O" or to last for four hours. The main idea here is to enjoy each other's company. This ought to be at the forefront of your mind all the time.

As such, you and your partner need to drop all of the expectations and focus on being together. That's all. All you need is to focus on the moment by savoring all of the emotions that come with enjoying the time you spend together. When you look at things from this perspective, you can't possibly go wrong.

Consider this situation:

Your partner's head is just not in it. They had a hard time at the office or perhaps some work-related problems. They are upset and can't seem to relax. Consequently, they just can't seem to enjoy themselves. Now, the worst thing you can do at this point is to assume that it's something related to you. In other words, take it personally.

Why would you?

Unless the issue is between the both of you, there is no reason why you should take it personally. Sadly, some folks think that they're partner isn't into it because they aren't attracted or don't like sex anymore.

This could not be further from the truth.

In this regard, it's important to take the pressure off as much as possible. In fact, there are times when you might have no choice but to just shut things down.

You may end up simply cuddling. There may be times when all your partner needs is reassurance. Sure, this sounds easy, but it can be really tough when you have your motor firing on all cylinders. In that case, you can make a game of it. Perhaps your partner might find it relaxing to watch you taking care of business yourself.

The point here is to eliminate pressure. Tantric sex is not the type of practice you can master when on the clock. Relaxation and focus are essential to making it work. Otherwise, it would be nearly impossible for you to find the way to ultimate ecstasy.

Please try to make sure that you have zero expectations when going into the bedroom.

How so?

If you enter the bedroom thinking, "I am going to have five orgasms today," then anything short of that will be a disappointment. If you change that attitude to "I am going to enjoy my time with my partner," then you are setting a different kind of expectation. You are focusing your mind on what truly matters, which is, enjoying the moment with your partner.

Relaxation is the key

Stress and anxiety are mojo killers. You don't need to be stressed out about anything in particular to kill the mood. The regular stress of day-to-day life is enough to bury arousal and pleasure. This is why relaxation is a fundamental tenet of tantra. You cannot expect to have a full-blown tantric experience if you are not relaxed and fully prepared to enjoy this experience.

Nevertheless, finding the ultimate relaxation isn't easy. In fact, it can be nearly impossible to settle down and find the right path toward peace and calm. Here is where you can see that tantra is not about sex. If you reduce your encounters to merely sex, then you are missing the point. Sex is the ultimate byproduct of the intimacy you have built with your partner. If you can't enjoy that, then you ought to reassess your priorities.

What to do if your partner just isn't into it?

At first, it might be really disappointing, especially if you are all fired up and they are not. This can be especially frustrating if you don't have much time to spend together. Yet, getting upset is the last thing you want to do. Instead, trying to foster an atmosphere of relaxation is key.

When you set the stage for your tantric encounters, you have any number of tools at your disposal. You can rely on a quick massage to help your partner calm down. Or, you can practice breathing in tandem. And then there's meditation. Often, just lying down together and guiding them through a visualization exercise can help lighten the mood.

Here is a quick visualization exercise that you can do with your partner:

First, lie in bed together. It's best that you don't cuddle or hold each other as you want your partner to settle down. But, if you feel inclined to do, then that's fine, too.

Then, sync your breathing. You can count out loud using the 1,2,3,4 technique. Take three shallow breaths and then one deep breath. As you exhale, try to picture the air leaving your lungs and floating off into space.

After, take your partner through a visual journey. You can describe anything you feel your partner will enjoy. If you want to describe an erotic situation, that could work great, as well. The point here is to help your partner calm down by using any means at your disposal.

If you happen to fall asleep, that's great, too. Just the fact that you fell asleep is signal enough that the experience was relaxing.

Ultimately, being patient with your partner is paramount to achieving the level of intimacy and connection you seek. Plus, who knows when you might be the one who needs a helping hand. In that case, your partner's patience would certainly be most welcome.

Being supportive and understanding

Perhaps the most important thing you can do when things aren't going too well is to be supportive of your partner. After all, if you weren't feeling your best, you would expect your partner to be understanding and supportive, right?

This is the reason why you need to focus on helping your partner feel as comfortable as possible, especially when things aren't going smoothly. In fact, just being there can be enough to give your partner the reassurance they need to feel better.

In contrast, if you get upset and make a big deal out it, then you can be sure your tantric session will go down the drain.

Consider this situation:

The male partner is having trouble getting an erection. This situation can be a potential dealbreaker. That is true if your only purpose is to engage in penetrative intercourse.

But then again, what if you threw that out of the window?

What if you figure out other things to do?

This is where being supportive and understanding play a huge role. After all, the male partner is already under enough stress. So, removing the pressure and replacing it with understanding is the best way to make things work.

Now, let's consider a different scenario:

The female partner can't seem to focus. Things are going as planned, but she just can't seem to settle down enough to reach the big "O." It seems that no matter how much effort is put into, she just can't seem to get there. This can be common especially in situations of high emotional stress.

So, the male partner, rather than feeling disappointed that his partner wasn't able to get there, can turn things around and help her relax. For instance, slowing things down by cuddling, kissing, and touching can all help reduce stress. Of course, this isn't a full guarantee that everything will suddenly turn around. But just being supportive and understanding is enough to get the female partner in the best possible frame of mind.

Please keep in mind that one of the core tenets of tantra is to help your partner reach their pleasure. While it is true that you are not responsible for their feelings, it is important to consider the vital role you play. You can be the guide that leads them down the path they need to take. All you are doing is facilitating the way. You are, by no means, the one who is responsible for their pleasure. As we have stated numerous times, this is a journey in which we must all go through. But your support, understanding, and patience are all key to helping your partner get the emotional connection you both seek.

It's a two-way street

Indeed, tantric sex is a two-way street. It's important to bear this in mind as "traditional" sex isn't always a two-way street. In fact, traditional sex is generally about one of the partners enjoying themselves while the other may, or may not, get something out of it.

This is very common when male partners are inconsiderate of their female partner's pleasure. By the same token, this can occur when females put unnecessary pressure on their male partner. As such, the female gets the attention she seeks while the male is under stress to perform.

These situations all reflect cases in which mutual pleasure is not the main focus.

Think about that for a minute…

When you are convinced that the goal of sex is to simply enjoy yourselves, you'll find that getting to the big "O" is not nearly as hard as you might think. But then again, the big "O" isn't the only thing you can shoot for. Just being there for one another is the most important thing that you can do to foster the intimacy you seek.

Ultimately, it all boils down to knowing that tantric sex is about giving and receiving. You ought to be cognizant of how important it is to play on both sides of the ball. When you are perfectly aware that it is just as exciting and pleasure to give as it is to receive, then you will uncover the true nature of tantric sex.

As a matter of fact, experienced tantric sex practitioners will tell you that there is an incredible rush that comes from seeing your partner reaching the heights of ecstasy because you led them there. The same can be said about the type of ecstasy you can achieve as a result of being with your partner. This type of satisfaction is unmatched.

Lastly, helping your partner find their ecstasy is not your responsibility. In fact, none of what happens in the bedroom is anyone's responsibility. This is what makes tantra so great; you are doing things because you want to, not because you have to. There is nothing that says that you have to help your partner reach the heights of ecstasy. Your role is to be the guide for your partner, especially when they are going through a rough time.

When you are able to do that, the level of connection that is built cannot be questioned. This is the type of rock-solid intimacy that builds strong couples regardless of whether they are in a committed relationship or not.

Chapter 15: Couples Ecstasy

By now, you are fully prepared to take intimacy to the highest possible level. This means that you are now ready to make the best of your experiences by sharing in the sheer pleasure that comes with enjoying time with your partner. You now have the tools to make the most of your encounters. This means that all you need is to take the time to put the exercises into practice. That is why we have stated multiple times throughout this book that the most important thing is to focus on what you are experiencing at the moment, the "here" and the "now."

With that in mind, this chapter is about enjoying tantra as a couple. However, this chapter goes beyond what we have already discussed. We are going to see how you can enjoy ecstasy as a couple, particularly during sexual encounters. This means enjoying some "Os" while also enjoying the pleasure which you can derive from your partner's satisfaction.

Taking turns

A common misconception in the world of tantra is that true mastery of tantra implies that the couple orgasms at the same time. While this is certainly an amazing feeling, the fact is that it is quite difficult to accomplish as men and women have differing rhythms. Consequently, you might be building up unrealistic expectations when assuming that you must both orgasm at the same time.

When looking at tantric pleasure, there is nothing wrong with taking turns. In fact, taking turns can be a rather liberating experience.

How so?

By taking turns, you are essentially freeing yourself up to fully enjoy pleasure. This means that you don't necessarily have to focus on your partner. You can let yourself go freely. This will open up the road to mind-blowing orgasms.

Of course, there is no need to feel guilty. This is hardly selfish as you are not taking your partner for granted. All you are doing is going with it. Then, you can totally devote your focus on your partner. This will allow them to experience the same kind of pleasure you have.

The opposite also works very well.

Perhaps you are inclined to pleasuring your partner first so that you can free yourself up for the big one. Ultimately, it doesn't really matter who goes first. The only thing that matters is that you are both on the same page. It could be that on one occasion, you hit the big "O" before your partner does. On another occasion, it could be that your partner gets there ahead of you. As such, it doesn't matter. What does matter is that you both take the time to make your encounters as pleasure able as possible.

There is one caveat to taking turns:

Please don't feel that you are entitled to receive or obligated to give. In this regard, taking advantage of your partner can be dangerous insofar as creating feelings of neglect. Your partner may feel that you are only taking advantage of them while they don't get their fair share. By the same token, if you feel that you are only giving and not getting your fair share, then try to avoid feeling resentful or even cheated.

The key here is to foster communication at all times. When you foster proper communication, you are giving yourself the opportunity to be on the same page all the time. This is especially important when something doesn't go right. Rather than blaming each other, you can figure out what didn't work right and seek to rectify it. Over time, you will get into such a groove that you won't have to think things through. You will know exactly what to do and when to do it.

Reaching the big "O" together

One of the most challenging things about tantra is reaching that big "O" in unison. While difficult, it is not impossible. All it requires is careful pacing and synchronicity. Some couple strive to achieve this ability. They feel that being able to reach that big "O" together, even after multiple "Os" before that, can truly foster the intimate tantric experience.

Now, if you don't reach that big "O" together, it doesn't mean that you didn't shoot through the roof. But by reaching the big "O" together, you can make the most of a unique experience that is quite uncommon among average couples.

Here is an exercise which you can do to help you reach that big "O" together.

First, it's important to recognize each other's rhythms and patterns. Generally speaking, one partner tends to reach the big "O" sooner than the other. This is regardless of whether it's the male or female partner. Although males generally tend to climax sooner than females. As you become aware of these individual patterns, you'll be able to recognize the pace for each partner.

Next, sync your breathing as much as possible. When the action gets hot and heavy, it can be hard to keep the same tempo. The partner that is getting closer to the climax will generally breathe a lot faster than the other. As such, the partner who is breathing slower must help the other to match the slower pace. This is helpful in controlling orgasm, particularly in men.

Then, as your breathing syncs, you can then match your movements accordingly. In particular, if you feel that you are losing control, slowing the pace of the game down is essential. As you match your movements, you can regain that flow thereby matching each other's arousal. As you feel the tension build up inside one another, you can increase the tempo as desired.

After, talk to each other. You can develop a code word to signal your partner where you lie. A color code is usually the easiest. For instance, "green" means things are going well but not quite at the climax. "Yellow" can be used to indicate you are close while "red" means you are getting ready to blast off. The goal here is for both of you to stay on the same color. That way, you can increase or decrease tempo as the color code demands.

Lastly, don't try to time the big "O." Most of the time, one will get there slightly before the other. In fact, many couples indicate that one's big "O" is triggered by the other's orgasm. In a manner of speaking, one's pleasure gets the other over the edge.

What could be better than that?

After the grand finale

What do you do following the grand finale is just as important as everything else that happened prior to it. Lots of couples enjoy lying in place when engaging in intercourse. They purposely make a point of not pulling out as this helps foster that intimacy between them. This is a perfect time to continue breathing in sync while taking advantage of the opportunity for kissing and touching. Many times, the emotions are so intense that it takes a while to recover from it. As such, pulling out immediately after the big finale tends to be a mood killer.

Once you have decided to pull out, it's important to savor the moment. While you might hear a lot of experts say you need to cuddle, spoon, or remain physically close, the fact is that it's up to you. You can choose to cuddle or perhaps just lie together. Sometimes, emotions are so intense that you're practically speechless.

Some couples like to shower together afterward. This provides even more opportunity for intimacy. Others would rather just cuddle up and spend time together. Others still like to spend some time just talking. You might find that these are moments in which you have the most heartfelt talks with your partner. This is why "pillow talk" has become synonymous with pouring your heart out.

Ultimately, it doesn't really matter what you choose to do. The important thing is to savor the moment with your partner. The last thing that you want to do is get up, shower, and get dressed immediately following a powerful moment.

Sure, you might experience some unusual feelings. There are cases in which folks mention that emotions get all stirred up, especially if you are going through a tough time. This can happen. But that's when both partners need to be on the same page. Often, you don't have to say a word. Just taking a minute to live the moment is enough to truly nourish your soul.

One final consideration

For those who believe that tantra is a set of rules which you must follow to the letter, they could not be farther from the truth. The fact is that tantra is a discipline which has a set of guidelines that you are completely free to mold in your particular means and ways.

After all, humans are all different. There is no question about that. The core issue lies in the fact that you need to discover what works best for you. This is why tantra is best practiced with a partner whom you have a relationship with. And while it's true that we have stated the fact that you can have a tantric experience with someone you have recently met, the best results come from practicing tantra with a partner whom you have full confidence in.

When you have full confidence in your partner, you are psychologically free to explore everything there is to explore your sexuality. To sum things up, anything goes! Yes, really, anything goes. This is why you need to go about finding what really makes you and your partner tick.

If you are into BDSM, that's fine. You can have a full tantric experience within the domain of BDSM. There is nothing in the tantra philosophy that says you can't engage in BDSM and have the full tantric treatment.

If your idea of having a tantric experience is to go out to a club and then hit the sack, that's perfectly fine, too. The point here is to find that balance that will help you reach the mind-blowing heights that you wish to reach.

For couples with kids and an overall busy lifestyle, reconnecting through tantra is a must. Try your best to clear your schedule, make time for each other, and just forget about the world. You don't need to run off on vacation for two months. Even a single afternoon can do wonder for your relationship. By being able to let go of everything around you, you can find the peace you need to really get in touch with your sexuality. Best of all, this isn't the type of practice you need to spend money on. You can set the stage in a very simple manner, have the house to yourselves, and have at it.

Tantra is about finding the zone that will eventually lead you to that impressive feeling of lust, connection, intimacy, and pleasure. In the end, you don't need to have a complicated set of positions and rituals. With tantra, what works for you is what works best. Please resist the temptation to compare yourself to others. They do what works for them. You do what works for you. Ultimately, this is the goal of tantra. In the event that you have multiple partners, then you will realize that different approaches work for different couples. As a result, becoming familiar with the person you are with is the fundamental axiom of tantra.

Conclusion

Thank you very much for taking the time to read this book. We hope that you have found everything you wanted to know about tantra and how you can make it work for you and your partner.

Now, you might be asking yourself, "what's next?"

If you haven't already started trying out the exercises we have laid out in this volume, then the time has come to do so. If you feel your partner is on the fence, talk to them! Ask them to read this book, too. It could be that they just need a little more information about the topic.

Once you are ready to try things out, the most important thing to keep in mind is to go slow. Don't rush things. The biggest mistake that couples make when starting out it to rush things. Allow things to flow naturally. Eventually, you will find your own rhythm. By then, you will have the experience you seek to find.

Please keep in mind that anything goes with tantra. As long as you follow the main guidelines we have set forth in this book, you will find the overall tantric experience to be the most rewarding of your life.

So, what are you waiting for?

The time has come for you to savor the most amazing sexual experience of your life. You will find that once you go tantra, you won't go back.

Thank you once again for taking the time to read this book. If you have found it to be useful and informative, please tell others about it. We are sure they too, will find it useful.

See you next time!

Description

Are you looking for a tried and true way of enhancing your sex life without all the gimmicks and tricks you find on the internet?

Are you looking for a way to spice things up with your partner but don't really know how to mix things up?

Are you looking for a way to improve your understanding of sexuality but aren't into BDSM or anything kinky?

Are you looking for a means of improving your emotional connection with your partner that's both holistic and natural?

If you have been thinking about any of these questions, then this is the book for you.

In this volume, you will learn about tantric sex and how it can help you find the perfect balance between you and your partner. In fact, you'll be surprised to find that tantric sex has been around for a very long time. Yet, many of us are yet to discover it. But when you do discover it, the experience you are able to unleash is unlike anything else you may have felt before.

In this book, you will learn about the following:

- The fundamentals of tantric sex and what it involves
- The role meditation and relaxation in tantric sex
- Exercises which can help you sync your entire movements
- The ways in which tantric sex can help you discover new levels of pleasure
- How to pleasure your partner while pleasuring yourself at the same time
- How to engage in sexual activity without thinking about "sex."
- How to foster intimacy and build mutual trust
- Making the most of the time you have with your partner so experiences are truly memorable
- Recommended positions that will surely leave you wanting more
- Discovering the ways in which orgasms can lift you to new heights

… and so much more!

If you are expecting a book filled with sexual positions, then you will be surprised to find that tantra is so much more than that. You will discover how the right mindset is fundamental in ensuring that you find the greatest amount of pleasure.

Also, you won't find a collection of "tips" on how to improve your sex life. You will find a treatise on how you can turbocharge your sex life so that it's the best that you can make it out to be.

These aren't just bogus claims.

There are claims made based on experiences and years of practice and study. In anything, you get the best of both worlds: philosophy and practice.

So, if you are ready to make the huge leap from a traditional sex life into the tantric way of life, then you have come to the right place. Take the time to go through this book. You and partner(s) will never go back to the traditional sex way of life ever again!

Come on, then, let's get started discovering the art form that is tantra today!

www.ingramcontent.com/pod-product-compliance
Lightning Source LLC
Chambersburg PA
CBHW070055120526
44588CB00033B/1440

WHISPERS FROM THE SHADOWS

MARYNTHEL WILLOWBROOK

HAGALAZ PUBLISHING

CONTENTS

1.	Acknowledgements	1
2.	Forest Magic	4
3.	Dreaming	46
4.	Spirits	76
5.	Seasons	89
6.	Magic & Moonlight	116
7.	Sorrow	138
8.	Shadows	151
9.	Wisdom from the Earth's Cauldron	169
10.	Old Gods & Messengers	222
11.	Becoming	252
12.	Discovery	294

ACKNOWLEDGEMENTS

This one is for my spiritual tribe, without whom this journey and, therefore, this book, would not have been possible.

Wendy Brown, Aura Mighton, Michael and Mary Whitcomb, Adriel, and Cernunnos, and as always, The Goddess, thank you for your love, support, and guidance. I wouldn't be here without you.

Thank you to Hagalaz Publishing for believing in my book. Thank you to my spiritual and support tribes, Wendy and Todd Brown, Aura Mighton, Michael and Mary Whitcomb, Natural Collective llc, Soul Empowerment, your encouragement and support have been immeasurable and I am grateful to each one of you. To Bob, for standing by me, always. To anyone and everyone who encouraged me to publish my poetry, thank you.

Poetry has flowed through me since I was a child. You'll find many poems about nature within this book, as it is my therapist, my sanctuary, and my heart's home. You'll find poems about old gods and ancestors and heeding the wild call. But in particular, you will find the story of a strange journey.

Several events in my life led me to seek my authentic self and my mission or purpose in this world. It screamed at me from the abyss, "Use your Gifts"! Little did I know, when I answered that call, and that when I lay down on that table for a past life regression, that my world would be turned upside down, and that I would need to rethink everything I thought I knew about life and who I am. Through that labyrinth of madness, of discovery, poetry flowed, trying to help me make sense of it all. I have only scratched the surface, and I know that what I know and believe today will be turned inside out again tomorrow.

Come down the rabbit hole with me. There's a potion on your left. It says, "Drink me".

A word on the cover imagery from Hector Prada

I first discovered this photography artist on Instagram, and my world stopped for a heartbeat or two. Something called to me from the mists of his images, pulling me in, creating a deep longing for something I couldn't name, and stirring memories as old as time. There was no stopping the poetry that this world evoked. I returned to Hector's images again and again for inspiration, and to satiate the yearning they had created. They were my muse. When it came time to put my book together, I knew what I needed the cover to look like and reached out to Hector for his approval. When he agreed, I danced with happiness, hoping that my readers, too, would feel the pull and be drawn into that other realm with me.

Thank you, Hector Prada, for the gift of your images to the world.

You can find Hector on Instagram @hectorprada83.

FOREST MAGIC

Echoes of Tranquility

Wandering the woods,

soul torn and breathless,

fleeing dancing lights

and flickering memories.

I fall weary and aching

to leaf-littered ground,

counting breaths

grasping handfuls of earth,

inhaling rich loamy fragrance,

until echoes of tranquility

return in soft waves

soothing discord

and easing fragments

back into place.

I am whole.

I am home.

Time with the Forest

She speaks in sunlight

and tells of splendid things—

dandelions and daffodils,

borrowed bridges

and fading shadows.

She weaves intricate stories

with poetic skill

like a gossamer web

shimmering with morning dew.

She quotes ancient rhymes

and creates her own poetic verse,

which she sings with joy.

I could spend days in her presence

drinking in her voice.

Oh, how I love my time

with the forest.

Woodland Bridge

Bridge to the silent wood,

carry me gently.

My footsteps are slow

and my soul is weary.

Lead me into the mist

of replenishing.

Heal my spirit,

for I would be whole.

Green Dreams

I've been dreaming in green again,

running through lush forests

teeming with life,

sitting in sweet meadows

dotted with wildflowers,

laying in springy beds

of soft cushiony moss,

feeding my soul,

finding my way

back home.

The Turning

Here among the ancients,

green-fringed breezes

speak of old things.

Wrapped in moss roots

curled and shadowed,

I listen with hope

seeking wisdom.

Stars ride the mist,

falling asleep on my heart

and I turn from the light.

Answers do not come.

There are none

this time around.

Sighs escape through

parted lips and rise

to be carried away

by forest song

creating new messages

for those who come after.

Tears fall and I sleep.

Canopy

Somewhere in the mists of time
exists a shadow space
where worries of the everyday
are easily erased.

Filled with forest magic
peace and solitude,
this is where my soul shines best
with lifting of my mood.

There is no substitute
for the work completed there
or the blessings of the trees
with their branches Winter bare
or full of green-hued life
protecting me from heat
as I contemplate the lessons
from my mossy woodland seat.

I live half my life in shadow

under canopy of trees,

while in rush of cold and darkness,

or relaxed with Summer ease.

Magic Lives Here

Another day well spent

among the mist and moss,

feeling the joy

that only happens here.

A single glimpse is all it takes

to know you stand

in the presence of magic

and wisdom pure.

Stand and listen—

absorb the essence

and you will be changed.

Taste buds

In the silence of the forest

I am transformed—

and it tastes like

love on my tongue.

Deep Forest Magic

Soft misty mornings

allow me to be

lost in the shadows

wandering free.

I play games of go-seek

with the enshrouded trees

but my joy gives me away

and they find me with ease.

These are the times

when a child once again

that I long to stay gone

from the world of men

and live out my life

without thoughts that are tragic,

experiencing only

deep forest magic.

Meeting the King

The Oak King stood in silence

surveying all the land

when I came upon him

to talk of all my plans.

But standing in his presence

my words all slipped away,

and I could not recall

what I thought I had to say.

And so we sat in silence

and shared our energy,

which reached my very core

and I wept openly.

Stumbling Upon a Forest Cottage

Come into my parlor.

Be my honored guest.

The trees and I are waiting

to serve whoever's next.

The table has been set

with fine china cups,

waiting for a traveler

to drink its contents up.

Steaming pots of tea

and frosted fairy cakes

will soothe your troubled spirit

and help you stay awake.

Unless of course you're tired

and would like to sleep—

we can provide a potion,

which causes dreaming deep.

Come into my parlor.

Drink, rest, or feed.

I'll do my very best

to supply just what you need.

True Form

The guardians stand watch.

His Majesty awaits.

All I need to do

is step through the gate

where I'll be transported

to a new time and place

and be one with those there

the fae-dryad race.

Untamed

I thrive in darkness

of forests deep

unhindered by rules of men

untamed and wild-free,

shadow-walking

glimpses of light

finding me

now and again

to remind me.

Queen of the Woods

If you're quiet

you can hear her

whispering

into the silence.

Pearls of wisdom

dropping gently

to those

who care to hear.

Soften your footfalls.

Quiet the inner dialogue.

Open your heart,

and you will be reborn.

Ancient One

I follow my heartbeat

to where you are

deep in the shadow-wood.

I know you'll receive me

take all my cares

and make me feel understood.

I curl my body and lay down

snuggled in your roots

where you take the pain away.

Wrapped in your essence

I am healed again

and I wish that I could stay.

Amergin

The first time I realized

that trees could talk back

was the first time I saw you.

You sang to me

and drew me

into your presence

and we talked of many things.

The first time I heard you

I was awestruck and afraid

that maybe I had lost it

and slipped over the edge.

But you took those fears

and you calmed them.

The first time I embraced

this strange magic

was the first time I knew

that anything is possible.

Moss-Drunk

Green thick air

fills me

and I am drunk

with moss

and lichen.

Vision blurring,

speech slurring,

I can only sit

and drink more.

Dizzy and clouded,

my mind thought-crowded,

it takes me to the edge

where I become

Other.

Patience

The Oak King stands,

Storm-scarred and silent.

Not a whisper will he share

until I wait ... in love,

sending him my energy,

healing and joy-full.

Then he speaks softly,

barely heard over sparrow-song

and hummingbird wing.

But speak he does,

and shares his golden light,

and I am humbled.

And grateful and filled,

full again.

Forest Guardian

Spirit of the forest,

wandering free—

tending with care

each leaf and tree,

filling them full

of loving energy.

This, her joyful mission

for eternity.

Whisper-Speak

Words drip slowly

from the trees.

Whisper-speak

with misty breath

caresses the senses

with dreamy softness.

Wisdom held silent

for far too long

is shared, breaks the heart

with its joy and longing.

Their speech is a gift.

Hearing is our gift in return.

Sweet Breath and Murmured Promises

Within the deep forest,

a portal of light opens.

Its sweet breath

reaches me from afar

and murmurs promises

of dreams fulfilled.

Fragrant mist swirls

in enticement

and I am lost

in its pull.

I'll see you on the other side.

The Dancing Tree

Twisted vision

of eternal beauty

in solitary pose

captured mid-dance

and frozen

within glass lens

in one perfect

moment of grace.

Oh, how I'd love to see

your entire choreography.

Test of Worth

Sleeping creatures wake.

Guardians of the forest rise,

testing my worthiness.

I am held in place,

paralyzed,

while they gather

and analyze

before I am allowed

to pass.

I am always grateful

for their protective insight

so I know

I am safe.

Meet Me in the Woods

Meet me in the woods

where the leaves fall

like the last breath.

We'll spin webs

of daydreams

that drift

like blue-grey smoke

and fill the sky

with silver threads.

We'll whisper poems

to the trees

and they will hold

our secrets

within their branches

until they become

new pathways

for those who come after.

Oh, won't you

meet me in the woods.

Forest Song

The forest

sang a song today

of richest melody—

the notes,

as crisp and sweet

as the first bite

of ripe apple,

rose on bird wing

soared o'er canopy

then dropped

into a stream

of liquid gold.

And I, mesmerized,

by the music

could do naught

but weep with joy.

Sanctuary

A castle created

from branches of trees—

a sanctuary

where I can breathe.

Fallen trunk altar

covered in moss—

a place to remember

those I have lost.

Solitude and silence

in sun, rain or snow—

When I need to replenish,

here's where I go.

I Leave My Bones

Mossy coffin.

Dream bed.

I will lay here

when it's time

to return.

I will leave

this body

as food for the forest,

and when milky bones

are all that remain

to show I walked here,

let the wolves

take them,

for I am of the forest

and I am no more.

Verdant World

In a verdant world,

dripping with mist and moss,

we convene.

Spirits of the forest

lumber slowly

and shatter the silence

with creaking limbs.

Thrumming in our blood,

the call pulls us forward,

a yearning in our souls

to gather in this place

once again,

to meet with and honor

Source.

We will always answer.

Never Alone

I saw you in the shadows

when I was alone

and then I remembered:

I am never alone

in the forest.

Morning Messages

Soft like rabbit fur,

the morning finds me

humming a secret tune,

whispering messages

to the flora and fauna

which dwell in the forest,

and feeling quite at home.

Best Friends

In a perfect world,

my best friends

would be trees

and we'd meet

in silly places,

talk of what we please.

Then go into town

and eat ice cream

for a treat,

or fluffy cotton candy—

spun clouds

of sticky sweet.

We would laugh and share

remembrances or

new discoveries

in a perfect world,

where my best friends

are the trees.

Nemophilist

Have you seen her

wandering misted woods

hair wild, and eyes haunted,

searching for something

that has no name

and may not exist anymore?

I thought to tell her once

that her search

may be futile,

and ask her, could I help?

But she stared

with faraway sight,

and so I remained silent.

Turning away,

I saw the mirror

and knew

she was me.

A Soft Place to Rest

If I've come too far

or have long to go

is a well-kept secret,

hidden from my knowing.

As long as the path

winds beneath my feet,

I shall place one foot

in front of the other,

embracing all that I meet.

Asking only in return

a soft place

of mist and moss,

now and again

to rest my bones

and refresh my soul.

Longing

I'm drawn to the mist

like a gypsy moth

to glowing flame,

tempting me

toward the unknown,

filling me

with a longing

that has no name.

Meet me in the

misty woods

and I'll show you.

DREAMING

Contemplation

Drawn to the view

framed in solitude

and lost in reflection,

my thoughts misty

like the landscape

from a vision

given in my slumber,

the meaning not yet clear.

They are frequent now,

these dreams of contemplation,

and I am often

left in wonder.

Sometimes answers find me

the moment I look away.

Sometimes I must dive

deep within to find them

but eventually

the answers come.

Steam Ghosts

Thinking to recover

my lost memories,

I sat down

with a steaming cup of tea—

but I could only watch

as steam ghosts

rose into the air,

whispering messages

of silent contemplation.

They Sound Like Shadow

Mist-filled thoughts

return to haunt me.

I love the dream

that sounds like shadow

and tastes like green.

I feel it in the whispers

and am lost in its embrace.

Let it consume me then,

and I will be at peace.

Capturing Mist

Dreamy images

with soft edges

float just beyond

understanding.

Trying to catch them

is like capturing mist.

Prism Head

I dream in iridescence—

rainbow hues of translucence

float and flit and settle

part of my essence.

And I remember.

Meteor Shower

I dreamed last night of broken things

while showers fell from high—

like crooked, dusty, twisted wings

as meteors went zooming by.

I bridged this paradox forlorn,

while the moon stared down on me.

One passed away while one was born,

and I wondered which was free?

Maiden of Mist

Another mist-swirled dream

filled me with longing

and when I woke

the fog remained,

pulling me back

into its comfort,

fueling the yearning

for which there is no name.

I gave in to its call

and am lost now,

destined to be

a mist maiden

for eternity.

The Mantra

Veils rise

with morning light—

cloudy visions clear.

This dream state

falls softly away—

meanings then appear.

I see

the world anew

reflected in a crystal sphere.

Speak the words

lest I drift away—

I am here.

I am here.

Astral Flight

Golden dream state

follows me through the day,

not truly in either world.

I wonder, what if?

But something

always catches my eye

and pulls me back

into one world

or another.

How long can someone

remain dreaming?

Interpretation

Dreams fall languid,

full of strange meaning,

questions about water

while flying through air,

and an odd set of challenges.

Answers come with reflection

and consultation

with those who see.

Unbound

In dream I soar

o'er misty glen.

Freedom unbound

flows through my wings

and I could stay

riding the currents

endlessly

in my dreams.

Lost Dreams

She weeps

in the morning

for the dreams

she lost

in the night.

Prophecy Stone & Tektite

My dreams are speaking

as I travel altered space,

stones held tightly

through my slumber.

They show visions:

some swirl in fog,

pieces lost in time,

some scream

their meanings

into my soul.

Most require meditation,

contemplation,

until understanding comes.

But I'll carry my stones

into this realm

and hope for illumination.

Shadow & Light

Drawn out

into the night,

let the darkness

seep into my skin

until I am naught

but shadow.

Follow the light

of the silver moon.

Bathe in her rays

'til I am light, once again.

Return to my bed

and let the dreams take me.

Silver, White & Purple

I dreamed of you

in purple night,

slowly dancing

'neath soft moonlight.

The vision came

in silver white,

and all the world

could see the bright

reflection of your

mystic flight,

and I was caught

in sheer delight

to have this chance

to reunite.

Rivers of Rue

Pieces of yesterday

haunt my morning

as tenebrous visions.

They follow me

dripping with

watery illusions,

creating rivers of rue.

Moon Dreams

Last night

I dreamt full-moon dreams,

and woke to

wisteria thoughts.

The Taunting

Drawn-in dreams

across worlds

in dusty hues

of silver and green

They taunt me

with lines

that waver,

surreal and shadowed,

until I am helpless

in their pull

and I forget

what is real.

Fog Entwined Dreams

The light called,

reaching through sleep fog,

entwining itself with dreams,

pulling her to the land of waking.

So she followed,

into another realm of vision,

soaked with hidden meaning,

and she believed new things.

Wind-Swept

I have drifted away

on silent smoke,

taken through dreams

of no meaning.

A blessed respite

from troubles

of broken humanity.

I'll stay for a while,

carried by the wind.

Returning Light

Cleansed by bright moonlight

from dark shadows creeping.

Travel through time

while my vessel is sleeping.

Dried ocean of tears

from unconscious weeping.

Joy and remembrance

are mine for the keeping.

The light is returning

through the land sweeping.

Healing and warmth

into everything seeping.

And I feel them taking

my heart with their leaping.

Water Clouds and Lotus Blooms

I was given a vision

of clouds on water

amid purple blossoms.

My reflection was missing

from the glassy surface,

so I could clearly see

the message held within.

Lost in the meaning,

hours I stayed

in lavender dreams

of lost days.

Beyond

Apricot visions

soft-clouded

and breath-stealing

fill my senses

and carry me

beyond now.

The Portal Tree

awaits my arrival

wondering

where I will travel

today.

Do You?

Do you dream

of faerie portals

in woodlands

deep and green?

Do you wish

that you could travel

to distant realms

you've never seen?

Do you know

that once you reach them

you'll want to stay

and not look back?

Then follow me,

my friend,

for I've discovered

the right track.

Forgotten Doorways

Another doorway

to another realm,

lost and forgotten

in modern shine.

It called me though

and led me here,

coaxing me backward

in time and distance,

reminding me,

daring me, to enter.

I'll tell you

the wonders within.

If I return.

Worlds of Dreams

Inside the fog of dreaming

there are worlds

within worlds

and you can't say

which is real.

A playground

for fantastic creatures

and things

that go bump

in the night.

It exists only

in dreams

and I visit

often.

Fountain of Truth

If I dreamed a million dreams,

I could never fill my heart ,

for I've walked the shadowlands

and I know what lies ahead.

In the center of it all

stands a fountain full of secrets

that she'll whisper in your ear

if you're brave enough

to venture just a sip.

Though it seems a simple task

to taste of crystal waters,

it is likely it will burn you

as it flows.

And the tree who knows the ending

and who always had the answers,

will look upon the scene

with sad regret

because the knowledge

that you're seeking

doesn't come to you easily,

and but a few will survive

the whole ordeal.

I have watched so many strangers

who think that they are ready—

but the truth, my friends,

is seldom what we wish.

SPIRITS

You Will Know

When I am gone,

you'll know I'm here.

You will smell my perfume

and hear me whisper in your ear.

You'll feel my chilly touch

as you lay in bed at night.

You'll see my silhouette

outlined in softest light.

I'll say the words that we agreed

so you'll have no doubt

and won't try to expel me

when you cast other spirits out.

I'll stay with you forever

or at least 'til it's your time

and we can be together

in the otherworld sublime.

The Crossing

Spirits speak

in foggy whispers,

echoing emotion

through the veil.

Loneliness lilting

among the forest,

softly sharing

their tragic tales.

Lovingly listening,

I share their sorrow

until unease

begins to wane.

Carefully crossing

their energy over,

finally freeing

them from pain.

Lost Souls

Insights rise

soft and mist-grey,

weaving stories

of earthbound souls.

They flow through me

like raindrops in candlelight,

shimmering

on the windowpane.

My Fate

Ghosts made of mist

haunt my waking dreams

as I wander empty places.

They wrap me in ethereal arms

with chilly embrace

strangely comforting,

evoking soft memories

filling me with serenity.

This is my fate, then.

I am content.

A Season

I wept last night

for things that are no more,

but reason returned

with the light of dawn,

and reminded me

that all is temporary.

We each have a season

and then we, too,

move on.

A Chance Meeting with the Unknown

In sleepless wanderings

I chanced to meet

the Unknown.

Draped in gossamer robes

of silver-white mist,

face shrouded in shadow,

she stood in silence.

An air of mystery

clung to her

like life itself

depended on its grip,

yet gentleness radiated

from her visage

and her presence was inviting.

I willingly accepted

her outstretched hand

and that has made all the difference.

Dances of Sorrow

Dancing with strangers

in the forest of forgetting

while meadow sage lingers

on the water's glass.

Waltzing them onward

through mists of remembrance,

then onto the violet flame.

Tangos of sorrow

spin in the moonlight,

then rise to another plane.

Anticipation and fear

mingle in rumbas,

and fear loses out in the end.

Perpetual dances

with beautiful strangers.

How could I do anything else?

Psychopomp

Dripping,

dropping,

footsteps falling.

Trekking,

tracking,

voices calling.

Silvering,

shining,

moonlight rising.

Crissing,

crossing,

no compromising.

Gliding,

guiding,

fear displacing.

Weeping,

wiping,

pain erasing.

Building,

bleeding,

duty fulfilling.

Listening,

leading,

dody chilling.

Resting—

now

it's done.

Searching for One More

Have you seen me

running

toward the water's

edge,

chasing cobweb

visions

through landscapes

of imagination,

ever and always

searching

for one more

soul

in need of directions

home?

The Trio

Black velvet surrounds

while lost souls fear.

The trio stands ready,

each with their part to play.

I whisper

'take my hand,

feel the love radiate

as light in the darkness.

Be afraid of nothing,

for all is well.

I let go, then,

and watch in awe

the exquisite beauty

of transition.

Silenced

Vision clouds

and heart breaks

with stories

told by those

who can no longer

share them.

Their voices

have been silenced.

And yet there is still light.

SEASONS

Reciprocal Blessings

Bittersweet blossoms

rustling leaves,

please bring me the blessings

my heart conceives.

In turn, I'll bestow

those blessings on others

'til love floods the earth

and hatred is smothered.

The Promise

The breath of Spring

begins with the softest inhale,

followed by a pause

and then she rains her beauty

down upon the earth,

washing it clean,

soothing thirsty roots

and filtering her sunlight

so that fragile seedlings,

born in darkness,

can ease

into the world.

'Tis a most gracious

and tender time of year

when the world

is full of promise.

Sweet Fever of Spring

I hear the voice of Spring

sighing on the wind,

stirring my heart

with restlessness,

warming my body

with sweet fever.

Balmy air tickles my nose,

smelling of promise,

reminding me

of wide-open windows

and hyacinth breezes,

until my soul cries out

with anticipation

and longing—

I am ready.

Bird Song

Spring breezes

sing songs

of eternal blooming

and all birds

know the tune

to sing along.

The Smile

Spring blossoms

reach a place

deep inside me,

and tickle memories

of sunshine and beauty,

fresh rain and flowers.

They squiggle upwards

and cause the corners

of my mouth

to rise.

April Showers

April rains fall,

soft or fierce,

warm or chilling.

She is a creature

of opposites.

Like me.

The Unfurling

Spring has finally arrived

where I am.

Tendrils begin to wake

seeking light and purchase.

Leaves have unfurled,

turning their faces to the sun

and I,

I am smiling.

Midsummer

Midsummer winds

carry feathery songs

through the woods,

which faeries ride

with mossy wings,

or catch with gnarled hand.

Some look like trees

dancing in dream-state,

reveling in the light.

There's magic in the air.

A Dream in Deep Summer

Searching for misty pathways

trapped in my memories

to cool my sun-baked skin.

Wishing droplets of sweat

from stinging salt

into sweet shadow-kissed

liquid heaven.

Just for this moment,

a small reprieve

is all I need.

Hello September

September came

with cool breath.

It entwined with

August's steaming heat

and transformed the air

into mist-swirled chill.

It left goosebumps

on my skin

like stepping from

high-noon sun

into forest shade—

and it was delicious.

Autumn's Gentle Sigh

She comes gently

with soft breath

held for long moments

and exhaled

in a sigh.

She feels the stillness

drawing nearer

and her pace slows.

She covers herself

with a fine quilt

crafted skillfully

in rich amber hues

and stitched with thread

shimmering gold in the light.

She will sleep soon,

but for now

she dreams soft dreams

and blesses the earth

with glory.

Orange

Some days

I dream in orange.

Pumpkin patches

and bittersweet blossoms

fill my vision

and carry me

to a land

of eternal Autumn.

Rhythm of Earth

October came softly this year,
with golden sun still warm
and shining his essence brightly
upon trees without Fall's uniform.

No heavy mist was present,
no chill was felt in the air.
If I didn't follow Earth's rhythm,
I'd not know October was there.

I'm confident she'll be coming,
her arrival not too far behind,
the day that marks her visit
on the calendar in my mind.

Symphonic Fall

The Autumn gala begins.

The first note rises

tentatively,

as if testing the air.

All quiver at the sound,

breath held.

Other notes join in

and the music swells

in perfect rendition

of forest symphony.

Light-footed,

tender-hearted,

he approaches,

hoping she will agree

to share this dance.

Tapestry

Fill me full of crimson.

Feed me bittersweet.

Cover me in saffron.

Then I will become part

of the splendor

that is Autumn's tapestry.

We, Too, Can Shine

Autumn came late this year.

So while tree branches

are normally bare and stark,

a stunning silhouette

against a watery sky,

they are still full of color

and have barely begun

to drop their leaves.

It is a beautiful reminder

that nature has her own pace

and that we too may shine

past what other's believe.

Luscious Darkness

Welcome November.

I love this month

because of its luscious darkness

and the beginning

of going within.

The howling winds

sing eerie lullabies

and dreams are taken

on their blustery wings.

All is shadow and

I am at peace.

Beautiful Scars

Russet and gold vistas

leave scars of beauty

on an open soul.

Deep emotion

and ancient remembering

live in these moments.

Those who allow

the magic in

cannot help

but be recreated.

Winter Dreams

Sugared skies call to me,

pulling me from deepest sleep

out of fuzzy blanket cocoon,

into breath tingling,

skin pinking

icy-tinged air.

And Oh, the dreams

that come after.

Letting the Ice In

Winter comes

and silence fills our souls.

A hidden place

between the shadows,

to sit a moment

with grief

and cover our tears

with snowflake.

We know this cycle

and know that

Spring will return,

but sometimes it's necessary

to let in

a little ice.

Faerie Kisses

Silver white silence

cocoons my spirit.

Lost in frosted thought

my feet wander

where they will.

White faeries dance,

swirling puffs of wind

that kiss my cheeks,

and I am content.

Winter Gods

Winter gods call me

to the wild places.

They soothe my troubled soul

with crystal flakes

and numbness.

They offer solace

as only they can.

Marshmallow-bundled,

I wait for their song

and offer my own

in return.

Winter Day Magic

Faerie-frosted forests

fill my soul with peace.

Freshly frozen footprints

offer sweet release.

Sweet silence surrounds,

allowing thoughts to roam.

Silver snowflakes settle,

icing my woodland home.

Misty melancholic memories

are free to go or stay.

Mystic magic manifests

on such a winter's day.

Sound of Snow

The silence of snow

fills me with peace.

Downy-feather flakes

fall from the sky,

blanketing the land

in soundless white,

enveloping all they touch

with magical hush

of glittering secrecy.

I love the silence of snow.

A Heartbreaking Realization

Scarcely have I understood

the depth of animus

that surrounds.

Walking frosted woodlands

searching for the answer,

my breath white.

Here am I healed.

MAGIC & MOONLIGHT

Abandoned

In restless dreams

I walk alone,

down high-arched halls

of steel and stone.

Melancholic music soars

throughout the lofty place,

while I wander aimlessly

this forgotten space.

What magic will I find here

or what answers lie within?

Time alone will show me—

let my journey now begin.

The Tarot Card

I drew a card

from deepest well

but the image

had been erased,

the meaning lost,

mine to determine.

I sought answer

within the tree.

Its spirits came

in numbers great,

solemnly delivering

ancient missives.

I knelt in awe

and gave my thanks,

then went on my way,

carrying the card

which now contained

new image and meaning.

Where are Stories Born?

Stories float on sunbeams

on mornings like this,

falling softly to rest

on the surface of water

untold, unheard, nevermore.

But if you happen to be there

at just that magical moment,

and you know the art

of listening—

truly listening—

you may hear the tale

riding on the rays.

You may write it down

or commit it to memory

and then tell a friend

who tells a friend

and so on.

And that's how stories are born.

Imagine all of the tales

never heard.

Trusting My Intuition

Fog-fueled

and bottomless,

introspection comes

in wistful waves

carrying me

on her wings

to a place

of inner knowing.

Here, intuition speaks

in that quiet way

that ebbs through

the fibers of my being

and illuminates

the right path.

Sometimes she shouts,

you know—

intuition, I mean,

startling me

with her thunderous message.

But this day

her voice sighs,

and it suits

the grey moment.

And I will listen

and I will heed

her counsel,

for she's not

been wrong yet.

A Prayer for True Sight

Sacred grove

illuminate my soul

that I may see

the deepest and hidden

traits and parts of me.

This is my will.

So shall it be.

Communion

A soft carpet of flowers

appeared beneath my feet,

as if by magic spell.

Soft as a lamb's ear,

white as new snowfall,

laid by the gods

to show me the way.

I followed, of course,

to sweet communion.

The In Between

I've stood here before,

so many times

between worlds,

between forms

not yet shifted,

not quite me.

There is no fear—

only a sense of peace

and true belonging

each and every time.

I cross the threshold

for I am

an in between creature.

Moonlight of the Goddess

Moon-lit moments,

reminiscent of freedom,

erase memories of pain.

Light fills from crown

down to toe-tip.

Goddess energy and love

courses through veins,

healing wounds old and new.

What joy and release

lies in a patch of light.

Potions

Magic elixirs

moon-full,

star-kissed,

apothecary.

Rare concoctions

smoke-fed,

wand-swirled,

wait patiently.

Joy Full Weeping

Who has soared the sky

when the moon is full

and the clouds sing

in riotous colors

of setting sun?

Who has carried stars

in hands full to overflowing

of sparkling delight

and thrown them high

to crown the night?

Who has wept in silence

for the sheer beauty

of being deliciously alive

and understanding

they are magic?

I have.

Shifting Shape

Magic hour comes.

Shedding this vessel

feels delicious

and tastes

like freedom.

The shift is complete.

Time to fly.

Transcending the Mundane

Awestruck moments

tear down walls

of disbelief,

fuel the magic within,

and remind us

there is more.

Full Moon

Darkness holds me

wrapped in comfort

while I await your climb

into the midnight sky.

Your light finds me

robed in serenity

at forest edge.

Here in solitude

we speak of secret things

and find joy

in each other's presence.

Gateway of Starlight

Stars fell like rain,

soaking me

with silver droplets

of light.

I stood silent,

drenched in their glow

while liquid luminescence

ran down my body,

creating pools

of shining gateways

I Travel Other Worlds

Shifting planes

to other realms,

where portal light

falls in curtains,

thick with mystery.

Webs spun

of iridescent threads,

sticky with anticipation,

ensnare thoughts

and weave them

into a vessel

for traveling.

What lies ahead,

though unfamiliar

and shrouded

in secrecy,

invites and compels.

There is only

one choice.

Changeling

I'm hiding in plain sight

but you'll never find me.

I've left my body behind,

an empty changeling thing

and the most real part of me

is far, far away in the Otherworld,

where this realm can't touch me.

I think I'll stay this time,

so be kind to the other me—

the one I left behind.

She's quite lost there.

Sky Fall

I thought

for a brief moment

that the sky fell

into my breath

while the moon

dried my tears.

I was mistaken

and all became silent

again.

SORROW

Rain Dance

Rain dances

a slow waltz

in my mind,

sweeping me

across forest floor.

Our rise and fall

is graceful and in time

with a silent tune.

Mist swirls

around our feet,

creating the illusion

of floating above.

It is beautiful

from a distance

and no one can see

the tears

of the rain dancer.

The Gifts

The mist is calling.

She sends missives

to your heart.

Fill your pockets

with melancholic moments,

drape sorrow

around your shoulders

like an ethereal cloak.

Slip heartache on

as well-worn shoes

and come to me.

Bring me these gifts

and leave them

that I may grow thicker—

And you are set free.

Suturing a Broken Heart

Beauty exists,

even in the face of sorrow.

We just have to lift our heads

to see it and let it in.

Small moments of healing

eventually string together

and stitch our broken hearts.

They'll never be perfect again,

but they'll keep us going.

If I Could

I've been searching

through the mists of time,

reaching out and calling,

but there is no answer.

Sometimes a faint whisper

floats to me in a single note

from a bird's song,

or in the sweet fragrance

of a falling flower petal.

I may catch a hint

in the fading ripples

a leaf makes

as it settles gently

on a pond.

But mostly,

there is silence,

and it's deafening.

I would save you

if I could.

But I can't find you.

Weary

She is weary

of promises unkept.

They wound her soul,

and yet

on and on she goes.

There exists a place

of pure beauty

where love rules

and vows mean something,

where the flow

is equitable

and heartache has faded

into the past,

where blame isn't placed

for pain felt

by broken bonds.

She longs for this world

and she can see

glimpses of its light.

So she toils,

tired and discouraged,

to finish the work

alone

so she can go

home.

Garden of Goodbye

She felt a deep yearning

to travel back to that garden

where her bleeding heart lay,

to taste the fresh dewdrops

that cut her tongue

with their sweetness.

She longed to spend

just one more hour

where goodbyes bloom.

Death of a Rose

Crumbling memories

cling together,

like brittle petals

of a dying rose.

They hold tightly

to life's stem

in beautiful disintegration.

Truth's Open Grave

Lost in breath of ashes,

time rolled endlessly forward

and tears turned to stone.

People and things were forgotten

and remembered

and forgotten again.

Judgments were passed

mostly without merit,

as is usually the case,

and truth fell

into an open grave—

as the world marched on.

She is on a Journey Back to Her Wings

Draped in sorrow's shadow

within a world

of her own making,

she waits alone.

Solitude becomes her.

Silence defends her

and she feels everything

to her very core.

The depths inside her

are unfathomable,

deeper than even she knows.

But she's delving

to find the bottom

and recover her wings.

Save Me

Weary and battle-worn,

upside-down and soul-torn,

feeling lost and forlorn.

I come to you at mid-morn,

where once again I'm reborn

and you save me.

SHADOWS

Truth or Dare

Blessed rays fall softly,

catching shadows unaware,

coaxing them from hiding,

to play a game of truth or dare.

The shadows will choose truth,

for that is what they are.

They will leave the daring

for the light that shines afar.

Though their way is seldom easy

and it could strip you bare,

they'll heal you afterwards

if you choose truth instead of dare.

Dark Creatures

She dreamwalks through beautiful

worlds of dark places.

She has no fear,

for she holds the secret.

The creatures here,

though perhaps considered odd

to the upper world of daylight,

she thinks are normal.

They, in turn, are friendly to her.

Few dare to enter their world

and fewer still embrace them.

They love her for her acceptance

and she loves them for their difference.

Hide & Seek

Light and shadow

play games with my soul,

pulling me in,

then hiding,

calling, retreating,

in a never-ending

circle of joy.

The Eternal Grey

Grey like my heart

wrapped in eternal shadow.

Mist-filled wanderings

leading me

ever onward.

Forward and backward

and in circles

to nowhere.

But always I'll follow

the misty pathway

before me.

Gnarled

Dark creatures call,

enticing me deeper.

They whisper grey things

with their papery breath,

cool and thin.

I listen and follow,

until I am no more.

Interaction with my Thoughts

I walk in shadow,

silver-drenched thoughts

roaming freely in my mind.

They drip ideas

and longings as they pass

unhindered on their way.

Sometimes I catch one

and nurture it

so it stays a while

and transforms

to become a poem,

but mostly

they run free

and I just enjoy

their dance.

Seeking Shadows

I walk at last light,

searching,

trying to feed

my insatiable

lygophilia.

I always find them

sighing their night songs,

whispering thanks

to the disappearing day.

And in this transition,

magic happens.

Shadow Touch

She felt the shadows

touch her,

sending icy shivers

down her spine.

In the silence

of the night,

they carried her

to their home

among the trees,

and she was seen no more.

Shadow-Born

Wandering,

mist-drunk.

Feeling

shadow-born.

Reaching

otherworlds.

Falling,

battle-worn.

The Graveyard is Calling

Day drifting

through shadowlands.

Cemetery calling

in feathery whispers.

Misty morning,

ethereal and damp.

Who will brave this world with me?

Disappearing Again

Soundscape of fog

swirling in darkness.

Bittersweet memories

laughing at pain.

Glass portal opens,

drawing on heartstrings.

She steps into shadow,

disappearing again.

Offering

Shadows dance

in rhythmic sway,

an ever-changing

panorama

to honor old gods.

I am blessed

that they would share

this sacred moment

with me.

I make my own offering

and add it

to the display.

Balance

Balanced

between light

and dark.

A dance

between lambency

and shadow.

Here I walk.

Esteem

And the light and the dark,

realizing all the qualities

they held in common,

bowed to each other

in eternal recognition

and respect.

She

She is a creature of the night,

a wisp of shadow

you might catch

out of the corner of your eye.

She is a soft murmur

barely audible,

words unrecognizable,

escaping in deepest sleep.

She is a single dewdrop

midnight-misty,

ready to evaporate

if you look too closely.

She is impossible to catch,

but if you're lucky

and deserving,

she may show herself to you.

Feeding on Darkness

Shadow spirit,

walk with me.

Lend me

your cool shade.

Feed me

the darkness,

that I

may know light.

Wisdom from the Earth's Cauldron

Carried Away

And with the sunrise

all is carried away

to float gently

to a new shore, where

contentment finds me.

100 Poems

I saw a sunset field

aglow in a wash of pink.

A garden of feathery stalks

bobbed gently on the breeze,

nodding their heads

and creating beautiful sounds

like a hundred poems

written to the sky

and spoken all together

in a symphony of eternal joy.

Spellbound

An in-between place

of serene contemplation

held me in its sway.

It sang a lullaby

of ancient origin,

hypnotic and sincere.

Vibrations of harmony

flowed up from my soles

and into my form.

Spellbound, I wept

for the exquisite artistry

contained in each note.

When silence returned,

I was indelibly altered,

and so I ever remain.

Waterfall Meditation

Shallow visions

hold me softly

within tender embrace.

Silky droplets

cascade freely

in death-defying race.

Meditative

state of being

created in this space

fills me fully,

eases sorrow,

and cannot be erased.

Earth Song

Lost in wonder

of the unknown.

I feel the earth's song

in every footstep.

Her melody lulls me

into deep trance

until we are one.

Where

Where does she fit

in this world,

her heart

a bleeding pomegranate

on the tree of life?

Golden Mirror

When the sky turns

into a golden mirror,

who can say

which is real

and which is

just reflection.

Sky Songs

I took a walk

among the clouds,

expecting perfect silence.

So I marveled

at the symphony

of sounds

discovered there.

Did you know

that clouds sing?

Wind sighs

and the sky hums.

The land below vibrates

like a tuning fork,

and it all sings

in perfect harmony.

The earth makes music

for those who would hear.

Carry Me

The sylphs dance

in a sunset sky,

weaving messages

within soft movement.

Sometimes they carry me

into the sky with them

to become part of their dance,

so I may understand

deeper truths.

In My Pocket

Amber light

falls in softness,

capturing this moment

forever in a golden cocoon—

I put it in my pocket

so I can remember.

Pixie Cup

Dainty and dew-filled,

the pixie cup waits

for the unsuspecting wanderer

to taste and tempt their fate.

'Tis only for the fae folk

to drink and know its magic;

for others who can't help themselves

the outcome could be tragic.

They look so very tempting

that one might not resist

the tasting of the nectar

as their heart and lips insist.

But I offer my advice

to protect you from yourself

and to keep you safe from vengeance

from faerie, gnome, or elf.

The sweet belongs to them

and they can be quite zealous

when someone takes their tasty treat

and they become too jealous.

Weaving Worlds Together

Dragonfly days

turn into

nostalgic nights,

softly weaving

silken strings

between worlds.

Flowing freely,

time disappears,

vanishing the veil

and inviting

sweet surrender

to its bliss.

Being Present

I walked a path,

steel-blue and silent,

lost in silver clouds

of memory.

But the earth spoke

in riotous purple

pulling me back

to this world,

to this moment,

and to the wonder

that is now.

Woodland Theater

Faerie tale stages

in unlikely places,

fill me with childish delight.

Foxgloves and sages

sharing wee spaces

add fragrance to the sight.

Here 'tween dream pages,

where my soul always races,

I am carried through the night.

Purple

Standing alone,

a long night having passed,

where magic was wrought

and lost souls were found.

Daybreak comes slowly,

a faint kiss in the sky,

its beauty replenishing

my spent soul,

and rewarding me

with purple.

The Storm Within Me

Riding on clouds

of storm-hued breath,

feeling the power

surging within.

Spilling release

in eternal struggle.

Electricity hisses

under my skin.

On the Shore of Misty Lake

Red berry dreams

float on white feather fringe

and carry me far away.

Lakes laced in mist

liquid light spilling in

put on a joyous display.

Here in this splendor

sitting soft-silhouetted,

I believe that I will stay.

Blue

I walked

with starlit heart

down paths of dirt

and memories

until I found

Blue.

With the Sunrise

Sweet morning light

fills the earth with bliss,

chasing away remnants

of night thoughts.

It rises slowly,

and the soul sings

as it is reminded

that all is choice.

New beginnings shine

and peace returns.

Shades of Purple

Violet footprints

lead to lavender doorways

where magic and memory

forever entwine.

Sweetness of orchids

wrapped in blackberries

scent the night sky

with fragrance divine.

This is where you'll find me,

bathed in the purple

and feeling like vintage wine.

Listen

The earth sings

her own heart-songs,

full of wisdom

and enchantment—

if only

we would listen more.

Return of Blue

Blue came back today,

no answer for where it had been

or why gone so long.

It just returned

and settled in,

as if no time had passed.

I thought to question,

seek answers of meaning,

but in the end

I just smiled

and settled in, too.

Falling Up

I fell into the sky today

amid ochre and opal streams,

swept-up tumbling,

upward falling,

tilting-turning,

visions coursing,

until I was no more.

Lightning

Lavender skies

full of white light

in painted rebellion.

I can feel its power

like breath on my skin,

standing hair on end,

causing blood-surge

until I am free,

touching the celestial.

Questions

Do you dream in color

with vivid sights and sounds?

Does the forest whisper secrets

as you walk its spongy ground?

Does the water tell you stories

as it dances on its way?

Do you stop and listen

to all it has to say?

Does the silver mist caress you

till you feel it in your bones?

Do you feel the nature spirits

telling you you're not alone?

Me too.

Microcosm

Under a mushroom

I lay for hours,

caught in wonder,

looking for past lives

among the bones,

but I only found

forgiveness.

The Blossom

Drenched in the softness

of greenest shadows,

light comes in

to showcase the beauty

of a single blossom,

lest she forget.

Taste of Color

Today the world

was a delicious green

embraced

by the glow of

lemon-yellow,

cotton candy-pink,

and a touch of

blueberry juice.

A color feast

for the eyes.

And you think

if you could

catch that flavor

on your tongue

for the briefest

of moments,

it would be

a delectable treat

bathed in sweetness

and tasting

like peace.

The Soul of Nature

I have wandered

deep into nature's soul

and felt my wild heart

beat faster,

or slow

in tune with her rhythm.

I have drunk

from the crystal stream

and felt my blood

hum her song.

I have spoken

with ancient trees

and knew their voices

were my own.

I have wandered

deep into nature's soul

and I have been changed.

Magic Dew

Dew drops of magic

glisten sweetly,

enchanting all they touch.

Transforming the ordinary

into a faerie tale

of wonder and delight.

Blessing those

with eyes to see.

Bluebells

Bluebell thoughts

fill my mind

and call me

to their woods.

Petite faerie blossoms

in bright dresses

dance and sway

to their own music.

I've tried to catch

the tune on the breeze

but the flowers

giggle at me

and that sound

is better than

any melody.

Stone Wall and Earth Joy

Leave me here

against the wall

where moss grows thick

and bathes my skin

in softness.

Take my breath

with the scent of earth,

deep and rich and ancient.

Cover my eyes

with shades of green

and brown and blue.

Caress my ears

with whispers of trees

and forest symphony.

Kiss my lips

with morning dew.

Leave its sweetness

on my tongue.

Fill my senses

that I may be complete.

Symbiosis

In dream I felt the earth breathe.

Its breath became mine.

I heard its heart beating

and mine thumped in time.

My tears watered its roots

in fellowship divine.

I now carry her song,

a melody sublime.

Breath of a Rose

Once, I dreamt in roses

and their whispered breaths

reminded me of

things I'd forgotten.

My waking was bittersweet,

for the memories faded

but their breath remained

and perfumed the air.

See the Beauty

Sweetness lies

in the simplest things.

One small glimpse

of pure beauty

can change your mood

into one of joy

and deep gratitude.

I find these moments

everywhere.

The Choice

Should I always wander

between thoughts of

moss-covered stairs

and the land

from which they rise,

torn between the two

and longing for both,

causing my breath

to expand

or stop

or catch—

Then what will

ever become of me?

Because that choice

will always be

impossible.

In Love

I've fallen in love

with a feeling...

the ecstatic awakening

of my soul-song

as I wander woodlands

deep and beauty-full...

that which stops me

and pulls tears of joy

from my heart...

a sudden wrenching

of emotion held tight

and pulled into

the light of day

and the incredible

sense of oneness

that always follows...

this feeling that has

dropped me to my knees

more than once

and turned me inside out,

and I am in love.

Night and Day

So goes the daytime

in glorious hues,

holding back the dark

with brilliance,

reminding us

tomorrow is another day.

So comes the nightfall

in deep velvet robes,

encircling the light

with shadow-speak,

reminding us

that it too is beautiful.

So stands the sentinel

to bear witness.

Soul Colors

Purple blossoms

color my soul

with dreams

of serendipity

and I am full

of gladness.

The Tree on the Hill

A small path through the flowers

leads me to where I want to be.

Sitting on the hillside

beneath a favorite tree,

breathing in the essence

of all that I can see.

Casting all my sorrows

to the winds, I set them free

and know deep in my heart

true serenity.

The Feeling of Beauty

Once I saw a castle on a hill,

a lone sentinel reaching for the sky.

The mist filled the valley below

and the sun filtered softly behind the clouds.

As I stood and gazed at this splendor,

something bubbled up from deep within.

Emotions that can only come from beauty,

a sense of wonder and belonging.

And I wrapped the feeling up like a treasure

and I've carried it with me ever since.

Star Song

Surrounded in silence,

I heard the stars

in operatic chorus.

The melody echoed

through the moonlight,

stirring the breeze

to cool my skin.

Transfixed, I stayed

until the last note

faded into darkness

and I moved on

with the song

etched on my soul.

Woodland Pool

Drawn inward,

compelled to this place.

Sugared drops of bliss

bathe her spirit

as they rise from

the woodland pool

in a misty mantle.

Sometimes

this is enough.

Under the Hydrangea

I went out to the garden

to see where the faeries live

and found myself,

quite accidentally,

inside a hydrangea.

I didn't remember shrinking,

or the growing of my wings,

but suddenly there I stood

under a sky of blue petals.

The other faeries, curious,

came out to meet me

and we spent a perfect day

among a jungle of blooms.

Pond at Sunrise

Light rises softly

in amber waking,

painting thoughts

with sweet music.

Songs of aching

float above

golden waters,

drowning sorrows

with melancholic tunes.

And I,

as witness,

turn to mist

and follow the ripples

into eternity.

OLD GODS & MESSENGERS

The Stag

Through the mists he came,

searching for me,

with a message

to deliver.

And in my awe

I didn't understand.

Owl Prayer

Beautiful spirit

of silence

and intuition,

guide my path today.

Lend me

your vision,

share whispered wisdom.

This is what I pray.

Raven Muse

You call to me

in the belly of the night

with messages from afar.

The ancestors speak

through your voice,

imparting wisdom

and foreshadowings.

I listen with intuitive ears,

hearing between the lines,

and then you are gone.

In the morning mist,

I call you my muse.

Rise and Shine

Elders rise

from ancient portals,

calling sleeping children

to rise and

shine their magic

into an angry world.

We must listen.

The Departing

Full of mist and wistfulness,

the forest calls my name.

'Tis time for the gathering.

All are here

in the form of deer,

and I take on the same.

We've come to bid farewell

to one of our own,

and lead him home

to the land of the ancestors.

The Flight

Symphony of love and light,

fill my heart with pure delight.

Help my weary soul take flight,

so I may soar when comes the night.

Free

Climbing out of the abyss,

preparing for flight,

the way ahead is shrouded.

Gossamer mist veils

the final destination,

but I trust the voices—

spirits of the forest,

spirits of the aether,

ancestors and old gods,

spirit guides of other realms,

lead me, each footfall directed...

I am divinely protected,

I am...

free.

The Download

Delicious delirium,

senses overflowing.

Transcendent transfer

filled with ancient knowing.

Vigilant vessel,

gratitude bestowing.

Call of the Stag

I have heard

the stag call.

I have followed

deep into the forest.

I have sat

at his feet.

I have listened

to his message.

I have reflected

upon his words and

I have understood.

Forever grateful,

I returned.

Precious Guide

You have been by my side

for lives beyond lives,

imparting gentle wisdom,

teaching the value of silence,

illuminating what is hidden,

guiding my intuition,

offering friendship,

nudging when necessary,

refraining when solo flight is required,

always comforting me with your presence.

For these, and so much more,

I thank and honor you.

Wildwood

Shallow breaths,

drawn from whispers,

send shivers

down my spine,

as I wander

misty pathways

seeking wisdom

from divine

beings of

the wildwood,

or the old gods

dwelling there,

my body trembling,

lifeblood stilling,

as I offer

them my prayer.

Night of the Owls

The time has come for flying.

No longer content

to be earthbound,

I raise my wings,

silent and sure,

and take flight

with my fellow owls.

There are journeys ahead,

duties and visions too.

I must answer their call—

see me soar.

The Guardian

She stands

before the guardian

within the mists of time,

awaiting her fate.

She holds no fear

In her heart,

for she has

stood here before,

and before,

and before that.

She knows what waits

on the other side,

and she is joyful.

Shhhhh—

the guardian speaks...

Petition to My Spirit Animal

Guide me,

sweet spirit,

through life.

Lend your wisdom

your magic,

and your intuition.

Light what is hidden,

show me the way.

For these I thank you,

for these I pray.

Spun Peace

Roots pluck light

from open hearts,

spilling grace and

bestowing knowledge

of old gods.

Their music spins

peace that rises

with the light.

Listen.

Lead Me

Lead me to old gods—
who dwell in secret places,
who meet me in silence
and replenish my soul,
who teach difficult lessons
with grace and reflection,
and serve to illuminate,
who are always within
to show the way.
Lead me to old gods,
where I can be me.

While Dreaming

Deep greens cover my soul

with a blanket of dreams.

Filtered light dances

behind my eyes,

the backdrop for visions.

This is my refuge,

a respite from wakefulness.

Here is where the old gods

speak lessons of worth.

Restore.

Release.

Remember.

Revive.

Return.

She is Here

Liquid gold light

falls in fractures,

creating a beacon

that calls to those

who seek.

The goddess is here—

she waits.

Snow Owl

She visits my dreams

with platinum-white glow,

bringing wisdom

and beauty,

like a full moon with wings.

The Glade of Gods

Sacred paths are calling

to where the old gods wait.

I travel to the secret glade,

step through the amber gate,

where filtered sunlight streams

to the path illuminate.

Here they share their power

and great magic we create.

Pools of Silence

I heard you calling

through the veil.

I came quietly,

like snowfall

on moss,

to answer

but my words

were lost,

an empty vessel.

The silence

filled me

to overflowing

and spilled pools

of ruby droplets

mixed with

my tears.

These Paths I Take

These paths I take

are solace,

a refuge

from the mundane,

from the angst,

from the world.

They offer balm

for wounded spirit,

silence

for troubled mind,

communion

with the divine,

and rejuvenation

for weary vessel.

These paths I take

save me.

The Narrow Path

I walk a narrow pathway

not meant for everyone.

The way is often difficult

but there are those

who would not see me fail.

Friends, soul tribe, guides,

gods and goddesses

stand ever ready

to lend a hand.

So I move forward

secure in their aid.

Returning to Wild

Copper and fire

meet in the shadows,

in a dance of sweet rebellion.

I don my wild heart

and throw myself

into the beat,

pure and ecstatic—

where together

we create

magic.

Murmuring Messages

Secret messages,

delivered in susurration,

dance to ancient drumbeat.

They fill the empty spaces

that cannot be named,

until their numinous truth

rises on wings of mist,

drifting evermore

to shadow folk

everywhere.

A Wish, Unfulfilled

I wander

in a world

of emerald and onyx

set in sterling.

Velleitie rises,

casting a shadow

on perfection

'til I am awash

in a sea of frustration.

I find my voice

and scream

with lover's rage,

an earthquake of pain.

The goddess comes,

a soothing balm

for my brow.

Soon my child,

soon.

Thundering

She's calling again

in deep sonorous voice

that rolls through me

like dark-storm thunder

rattling my bones,

tingling my spine,

racing my blood—

and I must respond

as I must breathe.

Path of the Goddess

She has walked here

many times,

her fragrance left

on the flowers,

her essence felt

on the earth,

until vanishing

into the mist.

I follow,

as I have before,

and before that,

for here is where

she speaks,

whispering

her truths

into my heart.

I will always

follow.

BECOMING

Marynthel

Named by others

Shimmering Mist,

Daughter of the Forest,

Otherkin,

Collector of Spirits,

Believer in Magic,

Ancient Intuitive,

Called to Old Ways,

Striving to Remember—

Reiki Attunement Vision

I am shown a misty cave—

I know not what it means

but a deep sense of loss

accompanies its leaving.

So many other images

create a visceral sadness

as they pass by my vision.

So many lives—

and I can't shake the melancholy,

the faint traces of memory,

they've left behind.

Portals

I've been traveling

through portals of late,

to realms unknown before.

Still in an altered state,

I return slowly.

Past Life Recall

"You were a wizard of time

in a past life," he said.

"That's why you don't feel

like you belong in this time

or any other.

You've been used to traveling

through them at will."

And suddenly, it all came together

and made perfect sense:

understanding is a powerful thing.

Time Cracked Open

The veil surrounds,

Mystifying,

carried on visions

of what has been

and shall be again.

Time speeds by

far too slowly,

with so much to do

before it's gone.

It cracks wide open,

spilling fragments

too far flung

to capture,

and the yearning

never ends.

I am Becoming

Creature of water

who needs no breath,

what name are you given?

Questions unanswered

begin to flow,

leaving more in their wake.

Red Crystal Skywalker,

I thank and bless you

for your guidance and wisdom.

I am becoming.

I Seek The Depths

Surface reflections

hold mystery.

Another world

lies within.

But my interest

turns to everything underneath.

Show me the depths

to satisfy my soul.

Memory

Things I cannot express

course through me.

Ancient places shown

leave tears of loss behind.

Are the memories mine?

Are they things yet to be?

Answers drip slowly.

Stardust Journeys

Portals and shadows

call me from this world,

leading me on journeys

of stardust and moonbeams.

There is rhyme and reason

somewhere

but they're hidden.

I am undone.

I am done.

Now, I answer.

Vibration of Remembrance

Papery voices pull me

to portals of light,

singing an ancient song

in soft harmonies.

I recognize the tune

from lives past.

It strikes a chord

deep within

vibrating through me.

I have no will

against its pull

and I am drawn

yet again

to previous realms.

Travel with Hecate

Stone hallways

filled with ghosts

rise in my dreams.

Ancient memories

like mist on water

haunt my nights.

They call me

to remember

who I am.

Colors of Impossibility

I dream in colors

that cannot be,

carried on light waves

of impossibility

to distant planes

of creatures unknown

shapeshifting with each

realm I encounter,

until I no longer know

which me is reality.

Finding Me

I was lost in the labyrinth of my past,

treading endlessly the path

of who they said I should be.

I was far from my base

in a land I had known

in past lives and recurring dreams—

when I found my way.

Now I walk a different path,

unique to me alone.

I have traveled very far

to reach here

but every single step

has been worth it.

How Do I Be Me?

Discovering portals

to worlds unknown,

down mossy trails

through the glen.

Becoming the creatures

who dwell in those realms,

with a thought

and the chime of a bell.

Who am I now,

dragon or gnome

or something different

I've yet to remember?

How do I return

to this mundane world

and still know

how to be me?

My Decision

Lead me to the doorway

but leave me standing there.

Whether or not I enter

is a choice I must make

and a solitary deed.

Who Am I?

Where do I belong

within this mixed up realm?

Not quite human,

not quite fae,

a tree-talking dryad

more at home

within the woods

than among 'my kind'.

I'm still learning

to navigate the earth

in this confining vessel

of skin and bone.

The forest is calling.

Soul Fragments

Running through mists

of time and place,

worlds and realms,

finding pieces

of who I am.

Struggling to fit them

where they belong,

so that I am complete

once again.

The Key Is In My Pocket

I've escaped—

bonds broken

and running free.

I slip the key

into my pocket

and I swear

I'll never forget

that I hold it

again.

Maybe, just maybe,

there won't be

a next time.

Bones of Steel

Gone are fears

and silver droplets

that fall from

red-rimmed eyes.

Carried away

on the murmurs

of ancients

they serve no more.

In their place

lives something deeper,

less yielding,

a spark fanned

into blazing inferno.

We can mourn

their passing

but there's work to be done,

and it requires

steel bones

and acid blood.

It is time.

Vortex of Endless Cycles

Drifting aimlessly,

scattered on the wind

in swirling vortex

of mysticism.

Memory overridden,

replanted dreams,

and the cycle

goes on and on.

A Creature of Opposites

Full of emptiness,

raging serenity,

thundering softly,

failing triumphantly,

conforming independently,

whispering raucously,

vehemently ambiguous,

purposely random,

echoing silently—

I am

swallowed

by grey.

Shifting Patterns

New layers

reveal lessons

still to be learned.

Shadows create visions.

Time to step back,

look at what truly is,

look at what has always been,

and shift the pattern.

Lives and Lessons

I fell out of time

and lives were washed away.

Broken pieces scattered,

glistening dust motes,

waterfall churned

their memories carried

to faraway seas.

My lives.

No wonder I'm lost.

The First Returning

I dreamed a million stars
in daylight of rainbow hues.
Translucent and fluid,
the sky flowed like water.

I knew this place
though I'd only just arrived.
A resonance deep within
cried out, 'Home'
in silent screaming joy.

My feet knew where to go,
and though the woods nearby
sang my return,
they led me away
toward the great gate.

Looking down I was not me,

though more me

than I had ever been.

Prismatic light radiated

from this vessel of shapes

color-full and gossamer.

I stared in wonder

seeing the world

through my skin.

There was more,

so much more,

but I cannot say yet.

I woke knowing

I had never been asleep.

Stained Glass Window

Looking through windows

of bright colored glass,

I feel myself slipping away

to places of future,

to places of past,

to places I long to stay.

Blink of an Eye

Other worlds call.

My reflection stirs.

I am starting over,

again and yet again,

shifting who I am now

with the mists.

I seek the silver mirror

so I may know

whether I am giant

or dwarf

or something other—

Whatever the case,

I will change again

in the blink of an eye.

Lemuria

Ancient memories stir,

born of stardust,

in a land of beauty

now lost.

Seed crystals speak,

imparting wisdom,

and I weep.

Reflection of Truth

Crystal reflections

show what is true.

I'm searching for answers,

following clues.

I'm walking new paths,

new thoughts filling my mind,

wondering and waiting

to see what I'll find.

I trust that all's well

and just as it should be,

and one day very soon

I'll know all that is me.

Cloud-Dropped

Dropped from a cloud

into the unknown—

What world is this?

What 'when' is it?

Which 'me' am I?

I don't think I belong

in this time or place.

Yet here I am,

dropped from a cloud.

So I do my best

to understand purpose,

to fulfill, and beyond,

to trust the powers

that reason is sound,

but it's no wonder

that sometimes I'm lost,

dropped from a cloud.

Flowing Secrets in Moon's Reflection

Shining stillness

calls me home.

Grand illusions

fall away,

flashing outwards

like lightning.

Secrets flow

toward forever,

reflected in the moons.

Transition complete.

I disappear in the glow.

Time Lines

I walk the lines of time,

seeking wisdom.

It lies in the depths,

and staying

on the surface,

avails nothing.

Time for a deep dive.

Will I Know

I've been falling,

drifting,

carried by the moon

through vortex

and rainstorm,

twisted and tumbled

until up is gone.

I find myself

wondering:

who am I now,

and will I know me

when I return?

Preferring Silence

Between the lines

we speak volumes,

silent as the depths below,

crashing over us

when momentum builds...

I prefer the silence.

Writer's Block

The words

have fallen silent

again.

How long this time

is unknown.

I won't chase them—

they'll return

when they're ready.

Until then

I shall continue

to journey

through the veil.

Restless Soul Syndrome

I have restless soul syndrome.

Not in some dissatisfied way,
where I'm not living my current life,
or always waiting for the next thing.

This is not the case.

I am aware, however,
there is more.

It's so close that I can touch it,
and travel there mostly at will
as it calls my name.

Great magic swirls there.

And the many other lives I've led

caress my memories,

drawing me

inexplicably backward and forward

at the same time.

The life I am in now,

and what it's about to be,

does the same.

So I find myself

in this moment,

and in so many others.

It makes me wonder sometimes:

what does one do

with restless soul syndrome?

Soul Pictures

Mist-ified...

Mist-erious...

Mist-ique...

Words fall like raindrops,

soft and malformed,

twisted slightly,

bent faintly,

painting new pictures

within my soul.

Bliss

Once I lived

in a hollow stump

overgrown with

moss and lichen.

Cricket song

was my lullaby

and bird twitters

my alarm clock.

Dew-heavy petals

gave their quarry

for refreshment,

and life was good.

DISCOVERY

Forest Wisdom

Leaf litter underfoot

cries for bare toes

that seek warmth

beneath their layers.

Mist-mellowed moonbeams

hold open doorways to other.

My time here

is almost done.

Less Traveled

I take a path less traveled,

in the footsteps

of Frost,

and he's right:

the difference

is tangible.

I meet few here,

but those I do

know that distinction too.

Some I walk with

for a time

and then we part,

either due to pace

or other paths we cross.

Some I walk with still,

and some

will be by my side

until my path ends.

But we are few

on this path

less traveled.

Unless

Early morning reflection

in soft, grey light,

weaves a story.

It tells an ancient tale

full of wisdom

and lost knowledge.

The loss it shares

pierces my soul

and I wonder:

when will we learn?

When will we stop

fighting each other

judging, using,

wounding, taking?

Silent tears

ripple the surface

of still waters.

I know

we are doomed

to repeat these lessons

again and again.

Unless....

Transition

Up in smoke it goes,

the illusion...

See beyond first impressions,

look for the hidden.

All is not what it seems:

why is this lesson so hard?

Guiding Light

A light in the darkness

to show the way,

to soften the lesson,

to remind us of the past,

to give a glimpse of the future,

to renew knowledge of true purpose,

to support and befriend,

to restore faith and meaning.

You are that light.

Thank you.

Hope

A small light

in the darkness

is all that I need

to fill my heart

with hope.

The Ghost of Yesterday

Yesterday's ghost

makes me linger

just a little longer

and I am

disappearing

into you.

Path to Peace

Silver laurel thoughts

edged in pastel cream

carry me through worlds

of falling stardust.

The sky whispers love,

that glitters the sea,

a path for lost souls

to remember peace.

Forgiveness

Forgiveness

falls deathless,

cascading

in firelight dance.

Healing

bubbles defenseless,

coursing

through lifeblood.

Love

unfolds openhanded,

seeking

darkness to dissolve.

Peace

is received.

Seeing Me

I dwell in possibility

where a realm of green

inspiration feeds the earth

and poetry falls from the trees.

It turns me inside out

with longing,

looking always for the key

or a new way

to help you feel

like me.

Or at least to understand

my yearning heart.

So I show you the magic,

the voices of the trees

and the beauty of shadow.

I lay open my spirit

and let it flow onto the page

like ink made of my blood.

And I hope

that some of you

will see the path,

will see my soul.

And that is enough.

Pause Button

I fall from a great height

into mist and shadow,

searching for the other side

where time is nothing.

I need to stop this endless march

just for a heartbeat or two

so I can catch my breath,

regain my strength,

rest my weary bones

before I journey on.

I do not need to quit,

just halt briefly.

Can you press pause?

No Excuses

Fragments of memory

touch my skin

like a kiss of grey.

The portal stands open,

promising to gather the pieces

into full recollection.

Knowledge comes

with a price.

Ignorance no longer

an excuse to

wait...rest...search.

The choice awaits:

the code word: reveal.

Here on This Path

Solitude finds me

here on this path

and I remember that feeling,

comforting, alone.

I wrap up its softness

around weighted shoulders

and they lift

lighter.

No words to pierce:

no need-to's

or should-have's—

It feels delicious

and lighter still.

I know

I won't be going back.

The Beckoning

Distant moons beckon

homeward.

I have been traveling

too long.

The time for returning

is near.

Elucidation

Golden light

echoes tenderly,

murmuring words

of perception

and understanding,

captivating my spirit,

searching my psyche,

elucidating all,

leaving me transmuted

and perpetually grateful.

Lost Boy

The lost boy

wandered deeper

into the woods

than he had ever been.

Stumbling and tired,

he came upon a lonely swing

hanging from an ancient tree,

where he sat down to rest.

Just as he got comfortable,

a gentle wind stirred

and the swing began to sway.

The boy took hold of the chains,

closed his eyes,

and lifted his feet off the ground

to enjoy the rocking motion.

He sighed at the cool breeze

on his cheeks and in his hair.

Just then a fierce wind

came whistling through the trees,

and the boy found himself

swinging wildly through the air.

For several minutes

he flew forcefully,

his hands aching and numb

from grasping the ropes.

The swing soared

high up into the air,

came down

and stopped dead.

The boy was gone,

and the forest smiled.

Password

Within a hill,

a doorway stands

that leads me to

all other lands.

The password you

must know and speak.

You can't use mine:

each is unique

and given you

when you were young

and you still spoke

the magic tongue.

If you can recall

that word so fair,

then find the door,

I'll see you there.

Dragon Ride

To ages past, I travel

carried on dragon wings

over mystical panoramas

of wild imaginings.

The secrets of the universe

unveil before my eyes,

urging me ever onward

through gold and azure skies.

The way has been opened,

though we know not journey's end.

Our spirit guides will tell us

when we should descend.

They'll lead us where we're needed

or where we're meant to be,

and perhaps we'll stay forever

in the mists of mystery.

'Tis Time

Lands unseen

feed my thirsty soul

and lead me

on journeys divine.

I only need go

when I can hear

the wind's gentle whisper:

" 'Tis time".

Trust

Deeper still,

I follow the path,

knowing not where it leads.

But I trust

it's the right way,

and I'm ready

for what's to come.

Leap

In vision I stand

in a realm of light,

misty green and life-full.

Swirling moss abounds,

carrying earth spirit

to accompany me.

This precipice I reach

is in the near future.

What lies below

I cannot see,

but I am unafraid.

Soon I will leap

or it will rise,

or both,

and I will be carried

to the next task.

This is my vision.

Last One

Surrounded in silence

of green-tinted brume,

I seek my ancient roots.

I honor the lives

that so far I've led

in spiritual pursuits.

I lay down my offerings

in humble gratitude

for their aid through my past.

Then offer a plea

that when this one ends,

it shall be my last.

Rescued

My feet climb to the unknown.

My breath glistens in release.

My hands carry wounded stars.

My womb cradles love.

My eyes shed salty tears.

My heart feels rescued.

Time

Time drips endlessly,

full of plans

and expectations

that we cannot fathom,

Now imprisoned,

for stealing moments

before they could slip away,

I await my sentence.

"No one was using them

anyway",

was not a defense

they said.

One day I'll gather

all the time

I've saved through my years

and I'll use it

for something really special.

My Purpose

The way is open,

invitation received.

No longer will gifts

be disbelieved.

Thankful, I stand

with heart open and ready.

Onward I travel

with footsteps steady.

What end to this journey

I cannot now know,

but I trust that the goddess

holds me in her glow.